GW00686355

# MEMOIRS OF THE GEOLOGICAL SURVEY.

## ENGLAND AND WALES.

### THE GEOLOGY OF

# SOUTHWOLD,

#### AND OF THE

# SUFFOLK COAST

### FROM DUNWICH TO COVEHITHE.

(EXPLANATION OF SHEET 49 N.)

BY

## W. WHITAKER, B.A., F.R.S., F.G.S., Assoc. Inst. C.E.

PUBLISHED BY ORDER OF THE LORDS COMMISSIONERS OF HER MAJESTY'S TREASURY.

LONDON:
PRINTED FOR HER MAJESTY'S STATIONERY OFFICE
BY EYRE AND SPOTTISWOODE,
PRINTERS TO THE QUEEN'S MOST EXCELLENT MAJESTY.

And to be purchased, either directly or through any Bookseller, from
EYRE AND SPOTTISWOODE, EAST HARDING STREET, FLEET STREET, E.C., or
ADAM AND CHARLES BLACK, NORTH BRIDGE, EDINBURGH; or
HODGES, FIGGIS, & Co., 104, GRAFTON STREET, DUBLIN.

1887.

*Price Two Shillings and Sixpence.*

Sei. het.
554.2
679ms
0 s. 49N

# NOTICE.

THE country represented within this Map was surveyed by Mr. Whitaker, with the exception of a small area of about a square mile, round Ellough in the North-western corner (done by Mr. W. H. Dalton and Mr. C. Reid) and of about two square miles at Kessingland in the North-eastern corner (by Mr. J. H. Blake).

The Cliff-section at Kessingland has been shown by Mr. Blake on Sheet 128 of the Horizontal Sections. It is, also, described in the Explanation of that Section, and will be referred to in greater detail in the Memoir on "The Geology of Yarmouth and Lowestoft." Only a brief summary of the facts, therefore, has been inserted here.

The cliffs of Easton Bavent and of Covehithe exhibit the finest known sections of the Chillesford Beds. The former also display the best section of the local condition of the shelly Crag. Both these sections, as well as that at Dunwich, well show the chief bed of the district, which is described in the Memoir as the "Pebbly Series."

The rapid wearing back of the cliffs, especially at Covehithe, is a point of interest; and the measurements now given will be of service to future observers.

The boring for water at Southwold is of importance, as it proves for the first time the base of the Crag, and the presence of the older Tertiary Beds beneath the Crag.

A list of publications on Suffolk Geology was given, by Mr. Whitaker, in the Memoir on the Geology of the country around Ipswich, etc. (pp. 134–151); 1885.

H. W. BRISTOW,
Senior Director.

Geological Survey Office
    28, Jermyn Street, S.W.,
        26th July 1887.

# CONTENTS.

# ILLUSTRATIONS.

PLATE. *Cliff-Sections.*

# THE GEOLOGY OF

# SOUTHWOLD,

### AND OF THE

# SUFFOLK COAST

## FROM DUNWICH TO COVEHITHE.

---

## CHAPTER I. INTRODUCTION.

### AREA.

The small area, only some 48 or 49 square miles, represented in the northern part of Sheet 49 of the Geological Survey Map, is wholly in the eastern part of Suffolk, with the one small town of Southwold.

Geologically this tract is in the London Basin, and it includes from 12 to 13 miles of coast, from Dunwich Heath on the south, to Kessingland on the north. Inasmuch, however, as the small area at the latter place, north of the stream, naturally ties on to that shown in the map to the north (67, S.), it will be described in the Memoir thereon, by MR. J. H. BLAKE. On the other hand, the southern end of Dunwich cliff (in 49, S.) will be described here, with the rest of that cliff.

### RIVERS.

The drainage of our district flows direct to the sea, by a set of small streams, without contributing to any of the main rivers of the county. Only one of these streams has open communication with the sea, and bears the name of River, the *Blyth*, which, rising in the district to the west (50, N.E.), flows into the sea just south of Southwold, after receiving on the north a tributary from Stoven and Wangford, and the short tidal Buss Creek, which isolates Southwold; and on the south (at its mouth) the joint streams from the valleys of Westwood Marshes and of Dunwich. The main stream is tidal in our district, up to Blythburgh, and, from the "Report from the Select Committee of the House of Lords on Conservancy Boards," (1877), we learn that its length is 18¼ miles and its drainage-area 71 square miles.

The stream that rises in the Drift near Wrentham and Frostenden flows southward and then turns eastward, joining the sea through the shingle of Easton Broad. A former tributary, south of Covehithe, is now separated, by the cutting-back of the coast.

The short stream northward of Covehithe finds its way to the sea, in like manner, through the shingle of Benacre Broad.

The longer stream, at the northern edge of the district, has its origin to the west (50, N.E.), its two branches entering our area at Ellough and near Sotterly, and the joint stream then flowing eastward to the sea south of Kessingland, where it would naturally filter through the shingle, but has an artificial outlet, Benacre Sluice.

It may be safely concluded that, in long-past ages, this last stream was joined by the short one just to the south; and further we may imagine that, a few miles out from the present coast, the Easton stream joined that system of drainage; perhaps also that the whole may have joined the Blyth, when the land extended many miles beyond its existing limit.

### Geological Formations.

No bed older than the upper part of the Crag either occurs at the surface in our district, or had been proved by boring to occur underground, until some years after the Geological Survey was made. There could be no doubt, however, from what has been found on all sides, that the London Clay underlies the Crag, in good thickness on the east, but thinning westward. The formations found are named in the following table, in which the right-hand column shows the divisions that occur at the surface, and are coloured on the map:—

It was not indeed until all but the last part of this Memoir had been written (except for the addition now to be made) that the existence of any bed below the Crag was proved, in this district, when, in the autumn of 1886, the boring for water at Southwold, after passing through a great thickness of Crag, pierced the London Clay and the Reading Beds. This boring, of which a detailed account will be found on pp. 78–80, has made certain what was before only an inference, and has enabled us to take our list of formations down to the Chalk.

| Recent | - | - { Coast Deposits | - { Blown Sand. |
|--------|---|------|-------|
| | | Modern River Deposit | Shingle. |
| | | | Alluvium. |
| Post-Glacial Drift | Old River Deposits | - { Loam or Brickearth. | |
| | | Gravel. | |
| Glacial Drift | - - - | - { Boulder Clay. | |
| | | Gravel and sand. | |
| | | Loam or Brickearth. | |
| ? Pre-Glacial | - Marine - | - Pebbly Gravel and Sand. | |
| Pliocene - | - - - | - { Chillesford Clay (or loam). | |
| | | Sand and shelly Crag. | |
| Eocene - | - { London Clay. | | |
| | Reading Beds. | | |
| Cretaceous | - Upper Chalk. | | |

The *Crag*, including the sand that has been associated with it, crops out along the sides of the valleys, and though occurring high up in many parts, on the south, is elsewhere confined, as far as outcrop is concerned, to low levels.

The *Chillesford Beds* also occur along the lower parts of some of the valleys.

The *Pebbly Gravel* forms the plateau of the southern and eastern tracks, sometimes reaching to the bottom of the valleys.

The *Glacial Sand and Gravel* occurs in the valleys in the northern half of the district, in some few places rising to the plateau.

The *Boulder Clay* forms the higher ground of this northern tract, occurring only in patches on the south.

The *Alluvium* of course forms the flat of marshy land bordering the streams.

The other beds are merely of local occurrence.

## SHAPE OF THE GROUND.

The district consists simply of a low plateau, chiefly of Boulder Clay on the north and chiefly of gravel on the south, which has been cut through in a very irregular way by the many valleys, and is sharply ended on the east by the cliffs of Dunwich, Southwold, Easton, Covehithe, and Kessingland, which cliffs are themselves separated by valleys.

The bottoms of the valleys have been filled by the deposits of the streams, forming the flat marshes that accentuate the slopes of the low bordering hills.

It is the cliffs which give geological interest to the district, from the sections they lay open to view, sections which, in the last three cases, are ever fresh, on account of the cutting-back of the land now going on.

As it will be convenient to describe each cliff-section as a whole, the usual stratigraphical arrangement in the following description will be broken through, as far as regards the cliffs. Otherwise the same course will be followed as in Memoirs on the neighbouring districts, the details of the Kessingland cliff being left for the Memoir on Sheet 67, S., to which they belong naturally.

## FORMATIONS NOT SEEN AT THE SURFACE.

### *Upper Chalk.*

It is not to be expected that one should learn very much of the Chalk from a small boring into it; but it is from such evidence only that one can learn one important point, the position of the top of the Chalk below the surface. Having now this knowledge at one place in our district, it may be profitable to compare the Southwold section with those in surrounding parts that give like information, and to work out the general slope of the Chalk-surface, underneath the old Tertiary beds.

When the Chalk is covered only by Crag, &c. its surface may be irregular, and therefore one cannot use the Beccles well-section for this purpose. Where, on the other hand, the old Tertiary beds have not been denuded from off the Chalk, the surface of the latter will be even, unless our district is an exception to the rule that holds elsewhere, which is very unlikely. Any curves that may occur in that surface are such as will be followed by the beds of the Chalk itself, being due to disturbance and not to erosion.

There are four sections available for this purpose, that at Yarmouth having been published many years,* whilst the others are more modern.†

Of course in all cases one must take the depth to the Chalk from the same level, that of Ordnance Datum being now usually adopted. The actual depth varies with the height of the ground, making allowance for which the Chalk is about 280 feet below Ordnance Datum at Southwold.

Throwing the data into the form of a table, we get the accompanying result, which may be summarized by the statement that there is a slight general dip in a north-easterly direction.

| Site of Well. | Position with regard to Southwold. | Feet to Chalk, below Ordnance Datum. | Slope of Chalk-Surface in Feet per Mile. |
|---|---|---|---|
| Orford Marshes, No. 1, about 2 miles N.E. of the town. | About 15½ miles W. of S. - | 218 | 4 towards Southwold. |
| Saxmundham - - | About 10½ miles nearly S.W. | about 80 | 14½ towards Southwold. |
| Bramfield (near) - - | About 7 miles S. of W. - | ,, 46 | 33½ towards Southwold. |
| Yarmouth - - - | About 20 miles a little E. of N. | ? 510 | 11½ towards Yarmouth. |

Since the above was written the following note of some trial-borings in Lowestoft Harbour has appeared :—" There was first a depth of about 20 feet of water, then gravel and sand, and finally the boring penetrated into the chalk."‡ Unfortunately the details seem to have been lost; but, in answer to my suggestion that a large boulder of chalk might have been struck, MR. LANGLEY kindly wrote to me as follows :—" We put down several trial-holes, and went well into the chalk, to be sure that we were in it; in one case 30 feet into the solid chalk. The chalk at the North Pier Extension is about 80 feet below high water." This unexpected occurrence of Chalk comparatively near the surface makes the slope of the Chalk-surface from Southwold to Yarmouth a less simple thing than stated in the table : it must be a rise of about 210 feet from Southwold to

* PROF. PRESTWICH, Quart. Journ. Geol. Soc., vol. xvi., p. 449.
† The Geology of the Country around Aldborough, etc., pp. 52, 53, and the Geology of the country around Halesworth, etc., p. 36. Geological Survey Memoirs, 1886, 1887.
‡ A. A. LANGLEY, Proc. Inst. Civ. Eng., vol. lxxxvii., p. 182 (1887).

Lowestoft, and then a fall, at a more rapid rate, of about 440 feet.

## Reading Beds.

Of the mottled clays and sands, which make up this variable formation, an exceptional thickness, for the East of England, occurs at Southwold. In the eleven other borings that, in Suffolk, pierce it from top to bottom, the thickness varies from about 30 to 50 feet, whilst in another boring, at Felixstow, at the southern edge of the county, it seems as if 61 feet may have been passed through without reaching the bottom.[*] Again, in the one Norfolk boring, that of Yarmouth, that goes through the Reading Beds, their thickness is 46 feet. At Southwold, however, they reach to over 70 feet, and, as would be expected, consist chiefly of clay.

## London Clay.

Although no fossils were found in this formation at Southwold there can be no doubt as to the age of the brown clay found between the Crag and the Reading Beds, that clay, except for the first foot and for the micaceous character of some part, being of like ordinary London Clay, and having the usual layers of septaria. The " basement-bed " was not well-marked ; but a few pebbles were found next above the Reading Beds.

Probably the London Clay occurs underground over the whole of the district, though ending off a little beyond on the west, where its basement-bed seems to have been found in a well at Bramfield (see Memoir on the Geology of the country around Halesworth, etc.).

---

[*] The Geology of the Country around Ipswich, etc. The Geology of the Country around Aldborough, etc. The Geology of the country around Halesworth, etc. *Geological Survey Memoirs,* 1885, 1886, 1887.

## CHAPTER 2. UPPER CRAG.

### GENERAL REMARKS.

THE beds that have been mapped as Crag in our district consist essentially of sands, sometimes ferruginous, sometimes light-coloured. These sands contain thin gravelly layers in places, and are sometimes crowded with shells, though generally unfossiliferous.

Some geologists perhaps would object to class great part of the unfossiliferous sand with Crag, and it is not asserted dogmatically that they belong altogether to the Crag: in the description of the Dunwich cliff-section it will be seen indeed that there is some doubt as to the topmost part of these sands. As a practical matter, however, that is from a mapping point of view, it is almost impossible to draw a line of division in the midst of a mass of sand that is of much the same character throughout, and no useful purpose would be served by the attempt to do this. Were one dealing with a very thick mass it might be otherwise; but it should be remembered that the difficulty in question is with only about 50 feet of sand.

The line that has been taken for the outcrop of the Crag is the base of the pebbly gravel, everything below which has been coloured as Crag, and, for the most part, I have little doubt but that this view is right. The absence of fossils is no more than should be expected in permeable beds open to the infiltration of water.

Of course in the northern part of the district, where the Chillesford Clay sets in next beneath the pebbly gravel, there can be no doubt about the underlying sand belonging to the Crag.

We are faced with another difficulty as to the Crag! The question arises to what division does it belong? There is none of the Lower, or Coralline Crag here; but the Upper Crag has been honoured with many names, and split up into sundry local divisions, so that one is forced to consider what these names and divisions really mean.

In the first place we may get rid of contentious questions that do not much concern us now. My colleague MR. H. B. WOODWARD has classed with Crag, in Norfolk, certain gravelly sands that have been known under the names Pebbly Sands and Bure Valley Beds.* These have usually been taken to be of the same age as the Westleton Beds (the pebbly gravel of our district); but insomuch as these beds are not here classed with Crag, there is no need to import them into the question of nomenclature. Again, one need not consider the Chillesford Clay, and whether it

* The Geology of the Country around Norwich, p. 31. *Geological Survey Memoir*, 1881.

is a definite bed or not, for here it has been regarded as definite. What one has to deal with is simply the nomenclature of the beds between the Chillesford Clay and the Coralline Crag.

This sandy mass, nowhere, at its outcrop, of any very great thickness, has been almost universally divided as follows :—

1. Norwich, Mammaliferous or Fluvio-marine Crag.
2. Red, or Suffolk Crag.

In order to reduce the question to its simplest form, it may be well to begin by getting rid of superfluous names.

The name Fluvio-marine was given because of the occurrence of some land and freshwater shells. Such shells are however of local occurrence only, and so rare, compared to the marine shells, that the name is really misleading, and should be dropped. MR. WOODWARD has already noticed this fact in describing the Norwich area.*

The occurrence of Mammalian bones at the base of the Norwich Crag, led to the name Mammaliferous being originally given ; but, as these bones are chiefly confined to one part of this Crag, the name is not a good one, and the more so as a like layer occurs at the base of the Red Crag, in which the bones are however derived, and phosphatized.

If the local name Suffolk is strictly applicable to any division of the Crag, it is to the Coralline, which occurs only in that county. This name, however, is rarely used, and practically one is left with the two names Norwich Crag and Red Crag, the latter of which is certainly unfortunate, as being based on colour, although that colour is rare in Norwich Crag.

Now it should be remarked that no one has ever seen the junction of these two. They do not occur together. It is in our district, however, that the question of their relation comes to the front. When showing specimens from this district the question "Do they come from Red or from Norwich Crag?" has been asked, to which I have answered that the questioner might take his choice, or, when further pressed, have adopted the not uncommon device of answering by means of another question, to the effect "What is the difference between Red and Norwich Crags: where does one end and the other begin?" and this question has ended the matter—it has never yet been answered.

There is a danger in prophesying; but nevertheless one may venture to say that it never will be answered ! A Norwich geologist, working southward, would probably claim our Crag for his division; whilst a Suffolk geologist, working from the south, would probably claim it for his. The fact is that this is a case, of a sort not uncommon in geology, in which too much value has been placed on slight changes of condition of deposit, which has led to divisions having been made where nature has made none. The Norwich Crag and the Red Crag are one; the former perhaps, to some extent, an upward continuation of the formation, but owing its slight differences to slight changes in deposition, the whole probably having been deposited in a short

---

* The Geology of the Country around Norwich, pp. 35, 36.

time, a time of no account in comparison with that taken by other formations.

I have not attempted therefore, in this district, to call the Crag either Red or Norwich: no useful purpose would be served in troubling about such a question. On the map the word Crag has been used alone, and here we should be content with the prefix Upper: indeed one may advocate the simplification of our nomenclature by the adoption of that term, which simply points to a geologic fact, and by the expunging of the names Red and Norwich Crags from the list of formations, except for local use. The term Upper Crag has already been used for the Norwich Crag Series by the Survey.*

Since writing the above, and whilst looking up the literature of our coast-sections, yet another name was found to have been used for part of the local Crag. The sand along the bottom part of Easton Cliff has been called the Chillesford Shell-bed or the Chillesford Sand; but there can be no good reason for separating this from the mass of the Crag below, and, as the base is not seen, one is left in doubt where the dividing line would be drawn, if it could be drawn. Two of our chief authorities on the Crag, PROF. PRESTWICH and MR. S. V. WOOD, Jun., having agreed in this question, it may seem a pity to disturb the arrangement, but in the interest of simplicity it is to be hoped that this name also will vanish, for one does not see what useful purpose it can serve.

From the tendency of the Glacial Drift to get to a slightly lower level northward, the Crag is lost to sight at the northern edge of our district, and in that to the north, in the neighbourhood of Lowestoft and of Yarmouth, it remains beneath the surface, except where sand is seen at the base of the cliffs, beneath the Chillesford Beds. To the north-west, at Beccles, &c. (in Sheet 66, S.E.), the out-crops mapped belong in part to those sands and gravels, which, though above lenticular laminated beds that have been regarded as Chillesford Clay, are there classed with the Crag.

The boring at Southwold has proved that the Crag there reaches to a depth far greater than would have been expected, in the absence of all evidence. No less than 147 feet of Crag were passed through, consisting of sands, sometimes with shells, and in one part with pebbles, the only exception being a bed of clay, 10 feet thick, near the bottom.

This is the greatest thickness of the formation yet recorded in England; and it is singular how well-sections have increased the record of thickness of this division of the Crag. Thus at Leiston, 60 feet have been passed through, without reaching the bottom, whilst, near by, at Saxmundham 105 feet of Crag were found, and, although at Bramfield the thickness decreases to 36 feet, yet at Beccles it reaches 80, including 12 feet of what is called Chillesford Sand.†

---

* The Geology of the Country around Norwich, p. 31. (H. B. Woodward).
 † The Geology of the Country around Aldborough, etc. The Geology of the Country around Halesworth, etc. The Geology of the Country around Norwich, p. 89, and Table opp. p. 156. *Geological Survey Memoirs.*

It becomes a question too, whether, in view of our further knowledge, some at least of the 120 feet of sands and clays in the Yarmouth boring that have been classed as Recent Estuarine Deposits,* may not belong to the Crag. One of the reasons given for that classification hardly holds, namely that " the level of the adjacent Crag is higher," there being no outcrop of Crag in that neighbourhood, and the Southwold section showing to what a depth Crag may go : some 140 feet below Ordnance Datum, or within less than 20 feet of the level of the base of the doubtful beds at Yarmouth. The clayey character of great part of these beds is certainly an anti-Crag feature ; but there is a bed of clay 10 feet thick near the bottom of the Crag in the Southwold section, and my former colleague, MR. W. H. DALTON reminds me that clayey beds were also found in the Crag, in wells, at Beccles and at Hoxne.†

MR. S. V. WOOD, Jun., in one of his many papers, questioned PROF. PRESTWICH'S classification and suggested that these beds might be part of the Glacial Drift, possibly " the prolongation of the Cromer beds."‡

## DETAILS.

In describing the sections the same plan will be followed as in other Memoirs referring to the Crag, the outcrop will be taken by successive valleys, up one side and down the other. Our most southerly exposures, however, do not belong to any of the valleys in the district ; that at the junction of Westleton and Dunwich Heaths belongs to the Minsmere Valley, to the south, and other two reach inland some little way from the cliff south of Dunwich ; but in none of these is there anything to note. The beds seen in the cliffs are described farther on (p. 52).

### Dunwich Valley.

The Crag seems to occur along this valley nearly to its head (in Sheet 50, N.E.), and on the right (northern) side it is cut far back, the junction with the overlying pebbly gravel being consequently very winding.

A pit on the eastern side of the lane a little south of Dunwich church (not marked on the map) and about a third of a mile W.N.W. of the ruined church on the cliff, showed (in 1880) gravel and sand, to a thickness of about 20 feet. Where clear, the lower part was mostly sand, and at one spot the layer of gravel at the base thinned out so that one could not divide the sand of the gravel series from the like light-coloured sand underlying it, which was seen to the depth of a few feet.

The sand is to be seen in places westward, and at the northern part of Westleton Heath the junction with the pebbly gravel was seen at the western of the two wee outliers of the latter.

Nearly three miles S. from Blythburgh, and at the western edge of the district, there is an old pit, on the eastern side of the lane, in which one could

---

* PROF. PRESTWICH, *Quart. Journ. Geol. Soc.*, vol. xvi., pp. 450, 451.
† " The Geology of the Country around Halesworth, etc." pp. 37, 38, *Geological Survey Memoir.*
‡ *Geol. Mag.*, vol. iv., p. 560.

see only sand on the eastern side, whilst on the west there was a little gravel over the sand, and by the lane there was a little stony loam (weathered Boulder Clay) at top.

The pit, ? lately disused (1880), a little N.N.W. of Brick-kiln Farm, and at the eastern edge of the common, is in brown bedded loam and sand, with some thin layers of grey clay, to a depth of over 12 feet. This loam is rather suggestive of Chillesford Beds, and is probably of Crag age, being below the pebbly gravel, from the wash of which the pebbly soil above the loam is in part formed.

At the farm itself, a pit showed the following section :—

> Pebbly soil, and light-coloured sand with pebbles (fewer in the
>    lower part) ; 15 feet or more.
> Light-coloured sand, without pebbles ; 7 feet seen.

Though the ending off of the pebbles was sharp, yet it seemed difficult to divide the deposits (between which the Chillesford Clay comes in elsewhere), on the supposition that the lower sand is Crag.

At the neighbouring Jointure Farm is another sand-pit ; and, a little beyond, is a heathy hillock, apparently formed by a scoop of the pebbly gravel into the sand, as shown in a pit.

The pit at the back of Bridge Farm, half-a-mile N.W. of the ruined church of Dunwich cliff, showed some 3 feet of pebbly soil (pebble-gravel ?) over light-coloured and brownish sand, in all about 25 feet. The top 3 feet of the sand contains layers of pebbles (? passing up into gravel); the rest of the upper part is false-bedded ; the middle part is rather coarse and darker than the rest, with small scattered pebbles and stones ; then comes finer sand, bedded with layers of loam or clay (of which there also a few above), and then sharp sand, the bottom part nearly all hidden by talus.

From here the valley turns northward, and has one side only, facing the sea.

About a quarter of a mile north-westward of Little Dingle the sand is loamy at top, which is suggestive of the coming on of Chillesford Beds.

A small pit at the back of Dingle House was about 10 feet deep, in light-coloured (whitish) sand, partly gravelly at top, and with a six-inch layer of grey clay in the middle.

The road-cutting at Great Dingle is in fine light-coloured and brownish bedded sand : the middle part very finely bedded, with thin loamy partings : near the bottom 2 to 3 feet finely false-bedded, with ferruginous and clayey partings.

## Westwood Valley.

At Great Dingle the Dunwich Valley is joined by that of the Westwood Marshes, which marshes are bordered by the sand that is here classed as Crag. On the right (southern) side there were no notable sections, and some doubt is thrown on our classification by the occurrence, just above the marsh-level, for more than half a mile, of clayey beds that seem to belong to the Chillesford Series (see p. 17), and which therefore should come at the top of the true Crag. Of course it is possible that these clayey beds have got into their present low position by some slight disturbance, or by lying in a hollow scooped out in the sand beneath. No evidence of either of these possibilities could be found however : and one was obliged to leave the question undecided, massing all the sand hereabouts as Crag as a mere matter of mapping-convenience. There is also another possibility, namely, that a bed of Chillesfordian character may occur some way down in the Crag, as well-sections seem to show. These points are noticed to show how difficult it sometimes is to come to a definite conclusion as to the exact position of many of these Upper Tertiary sands etc. The Geological Surveyor is obliged unfortunately to be a universal recorder, even of his own ignorance : he cannot ignore any part of his district, however troublesome it may be.

Although the sand is to be seen in various places (capped by a little pebbly gravel, by the roadside about a mile south of Blythburgh Church), but one noteworthy section occurred, at the sand-pit on the common just S.E. of Westwood Lodge, the highest (northern) part of which showed the following beds, in 1880 :—

> Light-coloured sand, somewhat gravelly, and with a thin, gravelly layer at the base; 0 to 6 feet; lying evenly on the bed below.
>
> Light-coloured sand, partly coarse, partly fine; the upper part with small stones here and there, and false-bedded; about 12 feet shown : much like the upper part of the sand of Dunwich Cliff.

The upper bed was thought to represent the pebbly sand, classing the lower with Crag. If this classification be right the dividing-line here is doubtful.

South-west of Walberswick the Westwood Valley joins that of Dunwich, at which place the joint valley must once have become tributary to that of the Blyth.

### *Valley of the Blyth.*

Up the right bank of our main valley the Crag sand appears only as a narrow strip, skirting the marsh, and interrupted in two places by the descent of the overlying pebbly gravel, etc., to the marsh level.

The railway cutting north-westward of Walberswick is in false-bedded pebble-gravel and sand, in the western part; but eastward there are sharp hollows, and one thin mass of the gravel over light-brown false-bedded sand, which latter may belong to the Crag.

Westward of the farm at the edge of Tinkers Marshes the junction of the gravel and the sand was again seen.

The short railway-cutting in the fir-plantation nearly a mile E.S.E. of Blythburgh church shows a gravelly soil over light-brown sharp false-bedded sand, like decalcified Crag, to a depth of about 10 feet.

The junction of the gravel and the sand is shown in pits at the little spur of the former about two-thirds of a mile S.E. of Blythburgh church, and about a quarter of a mile to the north-west.

The top part of the sand-pit in the corner of the roads a quarter of a mile S.W. of Blythburgh church gave the section shown in fig. 1, which represents a length of 10 yards, along a slight curve. The irregular junction of the gravel with the beds below, and the character of the latter, is suggestive of the sand being Crag.

#### Fig. 1.

*Section in a Sand Pit a quarter of a mile S.W. of Blythburgh Church.*

1. Gravelly soil, about a foot, passing down into the next.
2. Pebble-gravel, at either end.
3. Finely bedded brown sand, loam and clay (the last greyish), up to 3 feet. At the highest part (under ×) broken-up ferruginous pieces. [? Chillesford Beds.]
4. Light-brown sand, which goes down to the bottom, some 12 or 15 feet. [Crag.]

The Blyth valley now passes from our district, and the sections of its higher part will be found in the Memoir on Sheet 50 N.E.  We must cross over to its left side, along which, above the junction with the Wangford tributary, there is an outcrop of Crag sand, mostly of fair width, but with little in the way of sections, the only pit noted, about a third of a mile N.E. of Bulchamp Farm, being in bedded sand.

## Wangford Valley.

The narrow outcrops along parts of this tributary-valley are of more interest than those already described ; for here we meet with Crag in its shelly form, and in the absence of fossils the study of these sands is not of a kind likely to arouse enthusiasm, even in the most ardent geologic mind.

The first place in our course at which we meet with fossiliferous Crag is at the junction of the side-valley of Henham, where, at the bottom part of an old pit, now with cottages and gardens, S.E. of the road, by the edge of the marsh, nearly a mile N.E. of Bulchamp Farm, there is shelly Crag to be seen, with *Littorina littorea, Cardium edule, Mya, Tellina obliqua,* and *Balanus.*

Further eastward, at the corner of the spur, the junction of the pebbly gravel with Crag sand was seen.

The road-cutting down the hill (north) about half a mile S.W. of Henham Park Farm is in gravelly soil at top, over brown and buff sand, with a gravelly layer, and, lower down, a loamy bed (with gravelly iron-sandstone near, and another gravel-layer at, the base), the sand then continuing downwards.

I have no note of the occurrence of sections of shelly Crag up the Henham valley, or along the right bank of the main valley, by Henham Park, along which course only unfossiliferous sand was seen; but shelly Crag has been found in a well at Henham Hall (see p. 78), and Prof. Prestwich has noted the occurrence of " a similar but poorer group of fossils [referring to those of Easton Bavent] from sand-beds which are also below the Chillesford Clay."[*]

A small pit, which had once been larger, at the northern edge of the marsh about half a mile S.W. of Uggeshall church, showed irregular pebbly gravel, with sand, resting irregularly on false-bedded brown sand, probably decalcified Crag.  An old overgrown pit in the garden, slightly higher than the above, is in light-coloured sand, with pebbly soil at top.

A small pit at the edge of the wood about half a mile south of Uggeshall church showed a little sandy pebble-gravel, sloping down the valley, over light-coloured and partly iron-stained bedded and false-bedded sand (Crag).

A little S.E. of the house in Bullions Lane, half-way between Uggeshall and Wangford, there was a small pit in bedded sand.

A pit in a field nearly half a mile S.S.E. of Wangford church gave the section below :—

Soil and sandy pebble-gravel, up to 4 feet, resting slightly irregularly on :—
Whitish and buff false-bedded sand, with black grains in parts, and here and there a small pebble; up to 15 feet seen.  (?Drift or Crag.  Like the sand of Dunwich Cliff.)

We now reach our second exposure of shelly Crag, by the side of the marsh south of Wangford, where one of the pits has been noticed by Prof. Prestwich as presenting " similar features to the pit on Thorpe Common [near Aldborough], the beds being light-coloured and pebbly.  The common shells are *Cardium edule, Mya arenaria, Littorina littorea, Purpura lapillus,* and a few others."[†]

---

[*] *Quart. Journ. Geol. Soc.*, vol. xxvii., p. 346.
[†] *Quart. Journ. Geol. Soc.*, vol. xxvii., p. 345.,

There were three openings in this patch of shelly Crag when the Geological Survey was made, the first by the southern side of the road (and northern end of the wood) about three quarters of a mile below Wangford Church.

The next was near by, in an old pit on the eastern side of the southern end of the same wood, about seven eighths of a mile W. of S. of Wangford Church, where the section was as follows :

Sand and loam, ferruginous, with, at base
Sand and pebbles (some large flints), about a foot.
Shelly Crag, pebbly, light-coloured. *Cardium edule* plentiful.

The third, in a pit on the eastern side of the same field (by the western edge of the next wood), showed loam and pebble-gravel (Pa wash) over, and in pipes in, shelly Crag, light-coloured as before, up to 12 feet seen.

MR. E. T. DOWSON has kindly given me the following note of a pit " on Mayhew's Farm, Wangford," which is probably one of the above ; but having been taken in 1868 it shows some difference in detail, and also goes below the shelly Crag :—

Warp, a foot.
Gravel, 6 inches to 3 feet.
[Crag] { Shell-bed, 10 feet,
{ Sand, 3 to 5½ feet.

In 1838 SIR C. LYELL said : " I examined . . . . several inland pits of Norwich crag near Southwold ; and in one of these in the parish of Henham . . . . I picked up mammiferous bones and teeth from an undisturbed bed containing marine, freshwater, and terrestrial shells. Among the freshwater shells I found a species of *Cyrena*, which appears to be one of the varieties of that variable species, *Cyr. trigonula* [*Corbicula fluminalis*] found at Grays . . . . In each of the different localities of this neighbourhood [Southwold], as in those of the red crag of Suffolk, some shells are found which are not met with at other spots ; the whole assemblage, however, agrees very closely with that derived from the pits around Norwich."* Unfortunately, for the identification of this section, there was at that time no parish of Henham. Henham Hall was in Wangford parish. One is led to think therefore that we have here the first record of one of the pits south of Wangford. A like difficulty prevents me from identifying the section described by the REV. O. FISHER, who moreover cannot give me more precise information, not having fixed the site on the Ordnance Map. Probably he too refers to these pits south of Wangford ; but it will be best to quote his description, which is as follows :—" Proceeding [from Frostenden] to Wangford, we meet with pits in the true Norwich Crag, exactly resembling the deposit at Thorpe, near Aldborough, and at the pits about Norwich. It is a gravelly deposit of considerable thickness ; how thick the section does not show, because the upper part is denuded, but about 9 feet remains . . . None of the bivalves are in pairs. Here I found an antler of a deer, but too much decayed for removal."

" I dug in the floor of this pit and found the Crag to rest on a laminated sandy loam, closely agreeing with the upper part of the Chillesford Clay at Easton Bavent Cliff."† A letter from MR. FISHER, written in 1882, gives these further details of the section, as seen in 1865 :—

Soil, irregular.
Gravelly Crag - - - - - } 9 feet.
Sandy Crag (thin), with a layer of pebbles at the base }
Coarse yellowish sand - - - - - 3 „
Loamy sand with water, at the bottom of the pit.

It would be of great interest to know something further as to the micaceous loam or sandy clay into which MR. FISHER dug, and to find out whether it belongs to the Crag, or whether it may be London Clay.

MR. G. MAW ‡ has figured an irregular-shaped " Bleached patch in yellow ferruginous sands accompanying the Crag " in one of these Crag Pits, and he

---

* *Mag. Nat. Hist.*, n. ser., vol. iii., p. 316? (1839).
† *Quart. Journ. Geol. Soc.*, vol. xxii., p. 27. (1866).
‡ *Quart. Journ. Geol. Soc.*, vol. xxiv., p. 377.

remarks that these patches " are always surrounded by a zone *darker than the general colour of the sands*, and coloured apparently by the iron withdrawn from the lighter area . . . . These phenomena present two distinct points for consideration—first, simple chemical reaction and the mechanical washing out of the iron in a soluble condition ; secondly, the rearrangement of the colouring oxide, which cannot be explained by simple chemical and mechanical agencies."

Below this point the outcrop soon ends, the pebbly gravel going down to the marsh-level, for about three quarters of a mile, to beyond the entrance into the Blyth valley, along the rest of the right bank of which there seem to be but two narrow outcrops of the Crag sand, the pebbly gravel above coming down to the marsh-level for the most part.

The junction of these two deposits was seen in two places on the eastern bank of the side-valley south-westward of Reydon Hall, and again on the western side of the shorter side-valley just to the east.

The Crag is not again seen until it comes up at the foot of the Easton Bavent Cliff: but shelly Crag is said to have been found in great thickness, and but 10 feet beneath the surface, in a well at Reydon Hall, on the higher ground between the Blyth valley and that to the north (see p. 78). Many shells were found in it, but few were kept, the names of which are duly entered in the list of Gasteropoda (p. 82).

The small exposure of shelly Crag at Southwold, and the sections of the Easton Bavent Cliffs are described at pp. 61, 64, etc.

### Easton Valley.

In this valley five narrow outcrops have been mapped skirting the marshes, only the two near the mouth having a length of over a mile.

The first of these starts from the northern end of the peninsula south of Easton Broad, and reaches to Reydon Grove, north-eastward of which place sand is to be seen in a pit. At Reydon Grove a dry zone slopes up from the marsh on the north, and is succeeded above by a very damp uneven zone (? Chillesford Clay), whilst at the top the gravel and sand again form a dry surface, except for an irregular patch of stony loam. The damp zone cannot be crossed everywhere, but its water is mainly lost over the dry zone below. The outcrop of the Chillesford Clay would be only a line on the map, so that it cannot be shown.

On the same (right) side of the valley another outcrop occurs above and below Frostenden Brickyard, where sand has been touched (see p. 19). A small pit on the western side of the pathway, a little east of and almost joining on to the long pit at the yard, gave a section showing some peculiarity as regards the Crag sand, the beds being as follows :—

Chillesford Clay ?—Brown loam, up to 4 feet.
Brown and buff sand; 3 feet seen. At the top a layer of coarse dark brown sand, up to 6 inches thick; and gravelly. (Two large flints and a small boulder of basaltic rock, measuring about 9 × 6 × 3 inches, were found).

On the other, or left bank of the valley there are small outcrops of sand, westward and south-westward of South Cove. In the first of these the sand was seen about a quarter of a mile west of the church: it seems to rise up rather here, being higher than the Chillesford Beds, which skirts the marsh to both north and south. In the other the sand was seen, beneath the loam of the Chillesford Beds, about half a mile S.W. of the church, and it seems also to have been touched at the brickyard (see p. 20).

The last of these outcrops reaches from the turn of the valley southward of South Cove almost to the coast. In this we soon come to the little peninsula known as Yarn Hill, though without a name on the map, more than a mile due south from the church, a small pit in which is of some geologic interest.

The section was first described, in 1866, by the REV. O. FISHER, who says:—"Here is a bed of shells, chiefly *Tellinæ* in sand. It is covered by a brown loam, which I believe to be weathered Chillesford Clay, a band of flints in sand intervening;"* and he gives a list of the shells found, to which PROF. PRESTWICH made some additions in 1871.† In a letter, written in 1864 (to Dr. S. P. Woodward, and for which I have to thank his son MR. H. B. WOODWARD), MR. C. B. ROSE notices this pit, remarking that the Crag "is rich in the usual bivalves and *Littorina* . . . . and at its lowest portion contains the heaviest shells, *Cyprina Islandica*, and fragments of mammoth's bones."

Mr. S. V. WOOD says that the Easton and Yarn Hill Crag "points to a somewhat estuarine character, by the absence of *Mya truncata* . . . . and by the substitution for that shell of *Mya arenaria*."‡

The pit faces north and the section was as follows, in 1878:—

A little pebble-gravel, at the highest part, up to 2¾ feet.

Chillesford Clay.—Grey and brownish sandy clay, up to 15 inches.

Crag. { Sand : the top foot or so brown and somewhat gravelly, but this seems to die out westward : then yellowish-brown or buff, with a gravelly layer 4 or 5 feet down (on the west only, as far as could be seen); then a little mixed white and black (with light-brown under at the middle part)—in all 7 to 9 feet, not bottomed at the deepest part.

Shelly Crag, some 2 feet shown, towards the west, under the white and black sand. In this I found only one *Corbicula*, amongst a host of marine shells.

The pit has been worked further south, and at the south-east gravel seems to go down to a lower level.

It is to be noted that earlier observers saw more of the shelly Crag, MR. ROSE, in the letter above quoted, saying that "it is not less than 6 feet in thickness," whilst in 1868 MR. E. T. DOWSON saw 3½ feet, but only from 5 to 7 of the overlying sand.

Along the rest of this outcrop sand only was seen, in small pits, etc., at one of which, near the marsh south of Cove Farm, pebbly gravel, up to 6 feet thick, was seen resting irregularly on light-coloured bedded sand, up to about 10 feet shown. At the last the pebbly gravel seems to overlap, down to the coast.

### Covehithe and Benacre Valleys.

In the little valley southwestward of Covehithe there is a small outcrop of sand, from beneath the Chillesford Clay, which sand therefore must belong to the Crag.

There seems to be a like outcrop just north of Covehithe, in the valley of Benacre Broad.

Up the right side of the Benacre Valley there is a rather longer outcrop of sand round the spur north-west of the church ; but the mapping of this part is somewhat doubtful, as is noted further on (p. 31). Again there seems to be a small outcrop from beneath the Chillesford Clay about a mile and a quarter north-eastward of Henstead Church, and just in Sheet 67, S.

* *Quart. Journ. Geol. Soc.*, vol. xxii., p. 26.
† *Quart. Journ. Geol. Soc.*, vol. xxvii., p. 346.
‡ *Quart. Journ. Geol. Soc.*, vol. xxii., p. 538.

# CHAPTER 3. CHILLESFORD BEDS, OR CHILLES-FORD CLAY.

## GENERAL REMARKS.

This deposit consists of a more or less sandy clay, or sometimes a loam, or even a clayey sand, of marine origin; as in those few places where shells or impressions of shells have been found these are marine. It is finely bedded, generally micaceous, and clearly points to more quiet conditions either than the underlying Crag or than the overlying pebbly gravel.

When it occurs in force, as north of Southwold, it gives a good top line to the Crag Series, with which it is classed; for here it certainly occupies a definite horizon, as it does also to the south, whatever may be the case in some tracts to the north.* There is indeed but one doubtful spot in our district, elsewhere the Chillesford Clay being as definite a bed as could be wished for. The best sections anywhere to be seen are in the cliffs of Easton Bavent and of Covehithe (pp. 63–76), whilst at Dunwich the bed is absent.

Although the outcrop of the Chillesford Clay, in the valleys north of Southwold, has been mapped in separate patches, these of course are likely to be part of a continuous sheet, joining each other underground, except where the bed has been cut through by the denudation that has formed the valleys. Moreover it is possible that some of these also join at the surface, by an outcrop so narrow as to be unmappable, except as a line, or invisible from the wash of the overlying gravel and sand down the slopes. Where an outcrop has been shown on the map evidence has been seen, rarely from pits, more often from ditches, and generally from the clayey nature of the ground. It is likely therefore that further evidence may extend the outcrop beyond what was originally mapped, and it is not impossible that the same may be the case in parts of Norfolk, where the occurrence of the Chillesford Clay, as a bed in a definite position, has been doubted by some of my colleagues.

The absence of this deposit is owing, in some places, to its having been eroded before the deposition of the overlying bed rather than to its not having been deposited in those places: thus the pebbly gravels, next to be described, often rest very irregularly on the Chillesford Clay, to the extent of overlapping on to the Crag beneath. However, the original area of deposition of this division seems to have been much smaller than that of the sandy Crag.

## DETAILS.

### Dunwich and Westwood Valleys.

Just west of Dunwich one is led to infer the probable occurrence of a clayey layer on the southern flank of the valley, by reason of the growth of trees

---

* Memoirs of the Geological Survey. The Geology of Aldborough, etc., p. 25 (1886). The Geology of the Country around Norwich, p. 34 (1881).

(oaks). Can there be a thin representative of the Chillesford Clay here, below the pebbly gravel?

We now come to the doubtful spot (see also p. 10). At the brickyard at the southern edge of the marsh about two thirds of a mile S.S.E. of Westwood Lodge, the following section was noted:—

A little sand and gravel.

Chillesford Clay?—Sandy clay and loam; the top 3 feet or so grey and brown mottled, the rest more regular and bedded; about 5 feet shown.

Just east was a hole in sand, and the outcrop of the brickearth seems to end off.

At a somewhat later visit (1879) at one part, on the east, a little pebbly gravel was seen, at a higher level than the brickearth near by it on the west. On the other hand, both E. and W. of the brickyard there are small sand-pits (? Crag) at a higher level than the brickearth, as if the sand were above the clay.

The clay seems not to occur eastward of this brickyard, but it forms a narrow fringe along the edge of the marsh westward for about half a mile, when we reach the site of an old brickyard, the pits of which are ploughed over, and the section unrecorded.

I must confess my inability to account for the occurrence of the clay here, at this low level, when one would expect rather to find it high up the slope, directly beneath the pebbly gravel. It is possible of course that sands have been here mapped with the Crag, which have no right to that association, as noticed already (p. 10); and on the other hand it is possible that we may have here some lower and exceptional occurrence of clay in the Crag, an occurrence which MR. WOODWARD reminds me is not uncommon in Norfolk. There is no evidence of faulting or other disturbance, and indeed the only certainty is as to the presence of the clayey beds, which do not show in any other part of the Westwood Valley.

## Valley of the Blyth.

On the right side of this valley no sign of the occurrence of the Chillesford Clay was seen, except for the possible trace of that bed in the pit above Blythburgh, shown in fig. 1, p. 11.

On the left side but one very small outcrop was mapped, notwithstanding that earlier observers have noted the occurrence of Chillesford Clay elsewhere.

Mr. S. V. WOOD has figured a patch, by the high road northward of Blythburgh, and another eastward of Henham Park Farm.* PROF. PRESTWICH too says, "I consider there are indications of the Chillesford Clay on higher ground between it (Bulchamp Crag-pit, just out of our district, in 50 N.E.) and Wangford."†

In Section D. of his plate in Part I. of the "Supplement to the Crag Mollusca,"‡ the late Mr. S. V. WOOD, Jun., notes the succession, at the pit east of Henham Park Farm (alluded to by his father), as Pebbly beds over Chillesford Beds. I believe that he also noticed the presence of Boulder Clay.

Mr. WOOD having kindly given me a drawing of this section, as it appeared in 1866, this is reproduced in fig. 2, as a record of the facts observed,

---

* Quart. Journ. Geol. Soc., vol. xxii., p. 540, fig. 2. (1866.)

† Ibid., vol. xxvii, p. 345. (1871.)

‡ Palæontograph Soc. 1872.

and of his interpretation of them. He describes the pit as three furlongs E.S.E. of Henham Park Farm; but this must be measured from the northern end of the farm.

Fig. 2.

*Section formerly seen in a Pit eastward of Henham Park Farm* (WOOD).

About 12 feet to an inch. Section in a semicircle.

a. Clayey warp and humus. [Soil.]

[Pebbly Beds.] { b. Clayey sand.
  c. Pebbly gravel.
  d. Red and dark brown (almost black) sand, horizontally-bedded, with shingle layers.

e. Tongues of *f.* lifted up.
f. Laminated clay (Chillesford).

Mr. WOOD classed *c* and *d* as Bure Valley Beds, and *b* as possibly belonging to the same, though he was uncertain whether it might not belong to the Glacial sand, or even might be Post Glacial.

The lifting up of masses of the clay and the forcing under them of wedges of the pebbly beds is an occurrence of great interest, and shows how easily one might be deceived as to the succession of beds in a very short section. It seems to point also to some lapse of time between the two deposits.

At the time when this part was mapped the sides of the old pit, which is about a third of a mile eastward of the farm, were mostly hidden. At the central part there was brown loam, with some patches of Boulder Clay, from the weathering of which latter deposit the former has resulted, and with signs of gravel and sand beneath; but neither here, nor elsewhere in the neighbourhood, could one see any section in Chillesford Clay: indeed the pebbly gravel seems to reach to a lower level near by on the east and north, though this may be partly owing to wash down the slopes. There was certainly a dampness along part of the gravel-boundary, suggestive of a clayey bed beneath, and it is possible that such a bed might rise up, from beneath the gravel, at the pit, for one cannot see what other clay could occur in such a position. In the absence, however, of any certain sign of Chillesford Clay, it was unsafe to show it on the map.

The only outcrop that one was able to map in this valley and its tributaries is on the left bank, at the junction of the Wangford Valley, nearly a mile and a quarter S.W. of Reydon church, where a short narrow damp loamy flat separates the marsh from the rising ground of the pebbly gravel.

### *Easton Valley.*

Inland from the cliff at Easton Bavent there is an outcrop of these clayey beds round the peninsula south of Easton Broad, and also on the other (southern) side of what remains of the tributary valley; but the cliffs give the only sections (see pp. 63–67).

Above this, going up the right side of the valley, the pebbly gravel seems to rest on the Crag up to Reydon Grove (see p. 14), just westward of which place there are two very small outcrops of the Chillesford Beds.

Then the pebbly gravel seems to reach down to the marsh till just before getting to Frostenden Brickyard, whence there is a narrow outcrop of the Chillesford Clay to near the church, up the little side-valley.

At Frostenden Brickyard, which is about a mile S.E. by S. from the church, a long section, at the top part, from the barn eastward, gave the following succession, parts being more or less hidden :—

> Gravel, of more angular character than that below, filling a slight hollow in the sand, at the eastern end, up to 4 feet. This may be Glacial, though on the east it seems to pass into the sand.
> Pebbly gravel and sand, 3 or 4 feet thick by the barn : eastward replaced by, or passing laterally into, pale buff sand, with gravel-patches or layers : further east this sand, 12 feet thick, scoops gently into the clayey beds below : at the eastern end there was a mass of pebbly gravel in the sand, there darker and brighter.
> Chillesford Beds. Grey and brown (ferruginous) laminated clay, loam and sand, puckered at top sometimes ; 6 feet seen.

Another pit, a little south of the barn, and at about the same level, was some 8 feet deep in the last bed, here showing waves in sandy beds in the middle.

Further southwards, and at a rather lower level, a small pit continued the section downward, through about 6 feet of the Chillesford Beds, more sandy at the bottom, and passing down into brown sand, seen to a depth of 1½ feet (Crag).

I was told that, in the first pit, the clay had been worked through, to sand, the thickness of the former varying up to 12 feet, and that, in the lowest pit, the sand had been worked to the depth of 10 feet, when water was found.

For an earlier section at this brickyard, showing some differences in the pebbly beds, see p. 30.

On the west of the brickyard the mapping of the Chillesford Clay and of the underlying sand is uncertain, as there was nothing but sand was to be seen (presumably the upper bed), and moreover the map (old Ordnance), can best be described as crowded.

The small pit just east of the brickyard has been already described (p. 14).

The Chillesford Clay rises again on the other side of the side-valley, about half a mile S.E. of Frostenden church, and thence has a narrow outcrop into the main valley, up its right bank to Wrentham, and then down the left bank to Cove Green ; and another narrow outcrop reaches from just west of South Cove church down the left side of the valley to about a mile southward of the church, with a small section S.W. of the church (see p. 14).

Two small sections were seen nearly a mile and a little more than a mile eastward from Frostenden church, and S.W. of the Five Bells Inn, between Wrentham and South Cove, the pit of an old brickyard showed a little sand over the clay.

At South Cove brickyard, nearly three-quarters of a mile S. of S.W. from the church, the pit, open at the western part only in 1879, gave the following section :—

Pebbly Gravel, irregular.

Chillesford Beds { Fine, soft, light-brown, buff, and grey sand, somewhat clayey and passing down into loam, which, in its turn, passed down into the bed below ; 8 or 9 feet.
Grey and brown finely-bedded loam and clay ; about 4 feet shown.

One could not divide the more sandy upper bed from the more regular Chillesford Clay below.

Between the two drying-sheds a pit, some 6 feet deep, showed a wash of gravel and sand over grey finely-bedded clay, with sandy layers. Sand (? Crag) was said to have been found beneath the clay here.

At Yarn Hill (see p. 15), there seems to be a trace of the Chillesford Clay.

Along the very narrow outcrop N.W. of Easton Broad, clay was seen just below the Keeper's House and about a quarter of a mile eastward of it.

### Covehithe Valleys.

In the valley south and south-west of Covehithe a small outcrop has been mapped at Warren House, where loamy Chillesford Clay was seen, and it may extend further than is shown.

At the head of this valley there is a fairly broad outcrop.

The clay is cut into in ditches, as along the road about five eighths a mile from the church.

The ditch by the cottage-garden, north of the road, about half a mile W.S.W. from Covehithe church, shows a little gravel over Chillesford Clay. The ditch along the northern side of the lane westward shows the clay close to the surface for a few yards, and in that down the field southward there is a little capping of gravel close to the road, whilst the rest is wholly in the clay.

Along the valley north of Covehithe there is a narrow continuous outcrop of Chillesford Clay, except for about a mile at the eastern end of the left bank, where the pebbly gravel comes down to the marsh.

No good sections were seen; but only small cuts in loam, on the right bank just east of the Keeper's House at Chancel Cover, about a tenth of a mile east of Holly Grove, and on the left bank between the woods just north-eastward of the last, and by the corner of the track over a quarter of a mile west of Benacre Broad.

### Benacre Valley.

The difficulties found in mapping the right bank of this valley near Benacre are noticed further on, p. 31.

The Chillesford Clay borders the marsh from about a mile east of Henstead Church up to the Hall Farm.

At the eastern end of the outcrop mapped north of Benacre, northward of the church, something like Chillesford Clay was turned out of a ditch, and a little westward a junction of gravelly earth with loam was seen; but there was no good section.

In the little valley (E. and W.) that crosses the high road about a mile E.S.E. of Henstead, Chillesford Clay may be at or near the surface, judging from springs and growth; but no other evidence could be found, and therefore no clay was mapped.

The clay was seen nearly three quarters of a mile N.N.E. from the Hall Farm, Henstead; there is an old clay-pit about half a mile from it, in much the same direction; and nearly half a mile N.N.E. of it loamy clay has been worked to the depth of 10 feet.

Half a mile northward of Henstead church the Chillesford Clay again rises, and then skirts the marsh (just in Sheet 67, S.) to over three quarters of a mile N.W. of the church; but no good sections were seen.

The Chillesford Clay and the Crag (sand) S.E. of Hulver Bridge (also just in Sheet 67, S.) were hard to map. The out crop may extend to the eastern side of the little side-valley, between that place and the Parsonage; though nothing could be made out there but the presence of sand and gravel, very wet in the lower ground.

On the left bank of the valley Mr. J. H. BLAKE has mapped a very small outcrop at the spur about a mile and a quarter westward of Kessingland church, and a larger one, though still small, on either side of the hollow S.S.W. of the church.

# CHAPTER 4. PEBBLY SERIES.

## General Remarks and Literature

We have now come to what may be called the special formation of our district, as it is here, and just beyond, that it is most developed and takes up most space at the surface, reaching to the Minsmere Valley, just out of our district on the south, and up the valley of the Blyth to the neighbourhood of Halesworth, on the east.

It is for the most part a gravel, which, whilst chiefly consisting of flint pebbles, contains also many quartz pebbles (besides a few of some other rocks) and a small proportion of subangular flints. The whole has a sandy matrix, and there are often layers of light-coloured sand.

In two sections only, at and close to Southwold, have actual shells been found, the only remains found before the advent of the Geological Survey in the district having been casts in ferruginous beds. These shells are marine, and all the determined species occur in the Crag (see pp. 81–84).

This gravelly deposit usually rests irregularly on the Chillesford Clay or on the Crag (including the sand that has been mapped therewith); and it seems on the other hand to be overlain irregularly by Boulder Clay or by other beds of the Glacial Drift. There is no need, however, to make much of these irregularities, gravelly beds have a habit of coming in between other beds in such manner.

In the following notice of the opinions that have been published as to the age and classification of these beds, reference is made to such works only as refer in some measure to the district. This is hardly the place in which to take up the vexed questions of the Bure Valley Beds, and of the Weybourn Sands, of their relation to each other and to the Crag, and of the definite or indefinite position of the Chillesford Clay. Enough to say here that, pending a thorough re-examination of East Anglia, now that the Geological Survey Maps are published, I am not ready to accept all the conclusions to which some of my colleagues have come in Norfolk. It seems possible that anyone working southward from the northern part of Norfolk might get into a somewhat different mental groove from anyone working northward from the southern part of Suffolk. Both may be locally right; but it does not follow that either must be right generally; at all events the variety of opinion that has been evolved is rather bewildering. It is some satisfaction to say that any small contribution of my own has been in the way of simplification.

In 1866 Mr. S. V. Wood, Junr.,* classed this gravel and sand with his Bure Valley Beds, between the Chillesford Clay and the Weybourn Sand, the fossiliferous sand that overlies the Chalk in the cliff-section at that place, and which, on the other hand, is classed by Prestwich as Crag. Whilst classing the Weybourn Sand as Lower Glacial, Mr. Wood here leaves the Bure Valley Beds in an independent position.

The next year he stated that an examination of the fauna of the various beds, made with his father, verified the above order of succession.†

In 1868 the same author and Mr. F. W. Harmer‡ came to much the same conclusion, giving these beds the name Pebbly Sands and Pebble Beds from their character, that name being merely a synonym for Bure Valley Beds. As, however, the Weybourn Sand is never present where the Pebble Beds occur, it is suggested that the two may be mutually representative, unless the latter should be the uppermost member of the Crag Series. Farther than this the possibility is allowed of these beds representing not only the Weybourn Sand, but also the Cromer Till or Lower Boulder Clay, and the overlying sands of the Norfolk coast-section.

In 1869 Mr. Harmer recurred to the subject,§ saying that the only doubt that Mr. Wood and himself had, in connection with the Crag Series of Norfolk, was as to the identity of the pebbly sands of Belaugh and Weybourn with those of our district.

The next year Mr. S. V. Wood, Jun.,‖ classed the Pebbly Sand as Lower Glacial, but without special reference to our district.

The last of the three papers on the Crag by Prof. Prestwich,¶ which appeared in 1871, is partly devoted to the deposits now in question, to which alas! a new name is given, "The Westleton Sands and Shingle," from their marked occurrence near that village, just outside our district, to the S.E. Our author notices the likeness of the beds to those of Blackheath, which latter, however, in common with other Eocene pebble-beds, differ in containing flint-pebbles alone. If a new name were needful, I am sorry that Prof. Prestwich did not keep to his original preference for Southwold, as, by using the name "Southwold Beds" there would have been no confusion with the sand and shingle of the shore. In geological nomenclature it is better to use names of well-known rather than of unknown places. Again there is an advantage in using the loose word Beds, rather than more definite words such as Sand and Shingle; formations have a bad way of changing their lithological characters.

---

* *Quart. Journ. Geol. Soc.*, vol. xxii., pp. 547, 548.
† *Geol. Mag.*, vol. v., p. 190.
‡ *Geol. Mag.*, vol. v., pp. 452, 456.
§ *Geol. Mag.*, vol. vi., p. 234.
‖ *Geol. Mag.*, vol. vii., p. 19.
¶ *Quart. Journ. Geol. Soc.*, vol. xxvii., pp. 461-463.

In 1872 Messrs. S. V. Wood, Jun., and F. W. Harmer[*] emphasized their former conclusions, and definitely classed with the Bure Valley Beds both the Weybourn Sands and our own shingly beds, objecting to the new name given by Prof. Prestwich. It may be noted here however that Mr. Wood does not class all the pebbly gravel of our district together; but in various papers takes that of Dunwich and of Easton to be of later date, a conclusion with which I cannot agree, as will be explained in describing the cliff-sections (see pp. 57–59, 68–72).

These authors repeated in 1877 their conclusion of 1872[†] and Mr. Wood again stated it in 1880.[‡]

Mr. H. B. Woodward remarked in 1876[§] that the Bure Valley Beds "form a connecting link between the Pliocene and Glacial series"; but he classed them with "the Norwich Crag series," as far as Norfolk is concerned, though not specially referring to our district. He also noticed another name for these beds in Norfolk, to wit, "*Tellina Balthica* Crag," which was given because these beds, in the Bure Valley, are characterised by that shell.

In 1880[‖] I suggested the possibility that the pebble-gravel of our district might be represented by a like gravel which occurs on some of the Tertiary hills near London and westward, and I was glad to find that in the following year Prof. Prestwich came independently, and not knowing what I had said, to the same conclusion.[¶]

In 1882 Mr. H. B. Woodward[**] enforced his classification of 1876. To one of his statements I must take exception at once; it is as follows: "Nowhere, however, are such features [the lenticular or false-bedded character of the clays] better shown than in the coast-sections between Cromer in Norfolk and Southwold in Suffolk, where the "Pre-glacial laminated series" of Mr. J. Gunn exhibits many beds identical in character with "typical" Chillesford Clay, and in two if not more distinct horizons, etc." Occurrences such as are here described do not occur in our district; our Chillesford Clay can hardly be characterized as lenticular, or as false-bedded; nor, so far as is known, does it occur at two horizons (see however p. 17.) Whether it is typical or not is questionable: indeed one may object altogether to that term, not allowing that anyone has a right to fix a type for any deposit; such type-fixing being really only saying what Nature ought to have done at a particular period, according to the opinion of the founder of the type, any deviation therefrom being put aside as abnormal; a proceeding that is not at all in the mind of my

* Supplement to the Crag Mollusca, Part I., pp. xv., xvi., *Palæontograph Soc.*
† *Geol. Mag.*, dec. ii., vol. iv., p. 388.
‡ *Quart. Journ. Geol. Soc.*, vol. xxxvi., p. 464.
§ The Geology of England and Wales, pp. 290, 291.
‖ Geological Survey of England and Wales. Guide to the Geology of London, Ed. 3, p. 57. Repeated, with slight change, in Ed. 4, p. 60. (1884.)
¶ *Geol. Mag.*, dec. ii., vol. viii., pp. 466–468, and *Rep. Brit. Assoc.* for 1881, pp. 620–622. (1882.)
** Memoirs of the Geological Survey. England and Wales. The Geology of the Country around Norwich. pp. 31, 34; 1881.

colleague, whose object in making the remarks above-quoted was to guard against attempts at identifying various small isolated patches of laminated clays with the Chillesford Beds.

It should be remembered that the so-called "typical" development of any formation is really a matter of accident! It depends for the most part on where that formation has been first observed in detail, and this may, possibly, not have been in the place where it may be best shown or best developed. These remarks are made in the belief that attempts to fix on a certain condition of a formation as "typical" may have somewhat hindered geologic progress; and that it would be wise to abandon such attempts in future.

At p. 85 Mr. WOODWARD speaks of pebbly gravels that occur, in parts of Norfolk, *above* Lower Glacial loam, and he says that "these beds, with which the pebble beds of Halesworth, Henham and Westleton are correlated, are distinct from the Pliocene 'Bure Valley Beds,' which I group with the Upper Crag," to which one is disposed to say that any correlation of the Westleton beds with other beds that overlie Glacial loam is probably wrong.

At p. 105 a like occurrence, at Hardley, is noticed. Of course there is no reason why there should not be pebbly gravel in the Glacial Drift; indeed we know that there is; but because such a thing sometimes occurs in other parts it does not follow that our large spread of pebbly gravel is the same, especially as a very fair though thin representation of Lower Glacial beds sometimes occurs above it.

In the same year (1882) PROF. PRESTWICH[*] suggests the compound name of "Mundesley and Westleton beds" for everything between the Chillesford Beds and the Lower Boulder Clay; thus grouping with the pebbly gravels the presumably underlying series to which the name "Forest Bed" has (unfortunately, perhaps) been given. Into this question of grouping there is however no need to enter here.

This paper was criticised by Mr. H. B. WOODWARD,[†] who defends his own view, and also expresses his belief that the Westleton Beds are not of the same age as the Bure Valley Beds, a conclusion the possibility of which had occurred to me, as has been said elsewhere,[‡] though I do not follow the other conclusion, that the Westleton Beds are newer than the Lower Glacial Brick-earth.

---

As the gravel we are dealing with is blessed with so many names, each of which more or less involves a theory, or a classification, it has been thought best in this, as in the neighbouring Sheets of the map (49 S., 50 S.E. and N.E.) to steer an inde-

---

[*] *Rep. Brit. Assoc.* for 1881, p. 620.
[†] *Geol. Mag.*, dec. ii., vol. ix., pp. 452–457. See also "The Geology of England and Wales." Ed. 2, pp. 469, 505 (1887).
[‡] *Proc. Norwich Geol. Soc.*, vol. i., part vii., p. 210. (1883.)

pendent course, and to treat of the special locality only. The simple lithological name "Pebbly Gravel" has therefore been adopted, and in the Index of Colours, on each map, this division has been left unbracketted, either with the Glacial Drift above, or with the Crag beneath. The position of the gravel is thus rightly shown, without pledging ourselves as to classification.

This question of classification is one on which, I think, overmuch value is often placed. Whether a bed should be considered as the bottom of formation A or the top of formation B is often a matter of small importance, so long as one knows its true place in the geologic series relatively to other beds. Indeed, as regards such a question, in Norfolk and Suffolk, one has yet to learn where is the division between our Crag and our Drift, and is sometimes led to think that there is no definite plane of separation between them, except locally.

## DETAILS.

### South of the Blyth.

It is in this district that the pebbly beds take up most area (compared with other beds), forming the level hill-tops, except for sundry cappings of Boulder Clay, mostly very small; but being cut through everywhere by the valleys, which reach to the underlying sand, except in the case of that of the Blyth itself, in which the pebbly beds reach down to the marshes in three places, on the southern side.

The boundary-line between these beds and the sand beneath is of an irregular winding character, especially on the south, from Westwood, where it is at a rather higher level than in the valley of the Blyth and elsewhere, and is therefore more cut back by short side-valleys and combe-like hollows.

The old pits on and near Dunwich Heath show sand more than gravel, and in some cases it is doubtful what the sand may belong to. The descriptions of these are all given here, however, for convenience.

An old pit in a field about a third of a mile S.W. of Red House was overgrown and partly ploughed over when I saw it. There were signs of stony loam at top at the northern and southern parts. The middle part showed a little pebble-gravel over light-coloured sand; but at one part there was some clayey earth, and, in the bottom of the pit, some grey Boulder Clay, probably in a hollow scooped out of the sand.

An old overgrown pit at the edge of the Heath, about a mile S. of S.W. from the ruined church on the cliff, showed sand with a little gravel, and at top, in places, patches of loam. At the western end this loam was better seen than elsewhere, was stony, with some angular flints, and in parts became a clay. Clearly it is only decomposed Boulder Clay, but what the sand should be classed with can hardly be said. There have been pits in the field just north.

In a third old overgrown pit on the Heath less than a mile south of Dunwich House,* at the eastern end, there is pebble-gravel at top on the southern (higher) side; whilst on the northern side there is thin brown stony loam (decomposed Boulder Clay). A hole in the bottom of the pit is in light-coloured (nearly white) sand, with a thin clay-layer (= the sand next beneath the gravel in the cliff). At the western end there is, on the northern side, a

---

* Wrongly so called on the map. It should be Grey Friars House.

little Boulder Clay resting abruptly against gravel and sand (on the N.E.) ; and on the southern side there is again some of the loam at top.

Mr. S. V. Wood, Jun., gave me the following section of a clay-pit on Dunwich Heath, noted by him in 1864, which may possibly refer to one of the above :—

Warp. Of the nature of this Mr. Wood had no recollection.
Boulder Clay, like that of Sizewell (in 49, S). This Mr. Wood, at a later date, classed as Till (= Lower Glacial), 6 feet.
Sand bands, 2 feet.
Slate-coloured loamy sand, 1½ feet.
Red sand, 2 feet.
White sand, getting false-bedded about 5 feet down. Sand to the bottom of the pit.

What the sands belong to one cannot say, especially as the exact position of the section is not known. It is possible that Crag may have been touched.

At both the southern and the northern parts of the cliff there is a good development of pebbly gravel (see pp.53–56), and other sections, showing the junction with the underlying sand, have been noticed at pp. 9–11..

On the railway east of the Keeper's cottage, on the common north-eastward of Westwood Lodge, there is a long shallow cutting in sand, partly gravelly, with gravelly soil above.

Near by, the cutting through the common north-eastwards of Westwood Lodge begins, on the east, by the Keeper's cottage, in gravel and sand. Then, the ground, and the line, falling, the upper part is sometimes gravel (false-bedded) and sometimes pebbly sand, whilst below there is sand. Still further westward there is more of the lower sand, which then contains a layer of pebble-gravel, varying in thickness from a mere line to over a foot.

Besides these sections there are various small gravel-pits of no note.

### Northern Side of the Valley of the Blyth, including the Wangford Valley.

Some of our best sections occur in the Wangford tributary-valley, in the lower part of which the pebbly gravel is well-developed. Along the main valley also, below this, there is a broad spread, especially at last, when these beds form the plateau across to the Easton valley.

An old pit, in the Park, nearly half a mile E.S.E. of Henham Hall, is in this gravel, in which there is, at the highest part, a little iron-sandstone, up to about 2 feet thick, with casts and impressions of shells.

At the gravel-pit, marked on the map, over half a mile east of Henham Hall, between the former high road and the present one, the section was as follows :—

Gravelly soil.
Sand, up to 3½ feet. Noted as horizontal by Mr. S. V. Wood, Jun., in 1866.
Gravel, chiefly of pebbles, about 18 feet seen ; in the upper and clearer part false-bedded eastward, up to an angle of 25°. Mr. Wood has noted this "continuous oblique bedding."

Another large pit, also marked on the map, about two thirds of a mile N.N.E. of Henham Hall, gives a good section, and Mr. S. V. Wood, Jun., told me that he had seen here "25 feet of pebbles in one uninterrupted oblique stratification."

Just above (westward) of this the Boulder Clay sweeps down to the stream-level, for a short way ; but in the tongue of clay there are three small hummocks of the pebbly beds.

On the other (left) side of this tributary-valley the outcrop is narrow to below Wangford, when it again broadens, and until reaching that village no notable section occurs, though the mapping is not without evidence.

E 50061. C

The gravel-pit just S.W. of the windmill on the high road N.E. of
Wangford village, and about a quarter of a mile from the church, gave a
somewhat peculiar section, unlike any other in the neighbourhood, and
showing, I believe, Glacial gravel irregularly overlying the pebbly gravel.
The junction was not to be seen on my first visit, in 1878, but two years later
the part at the western end had been freshly cut, enabling me to lay bare the
junction, and to make the sketch of which Fig. 3 is a copy.

Fig. 3.

*Section in a Gravel Pit N.E. of Wangford.*

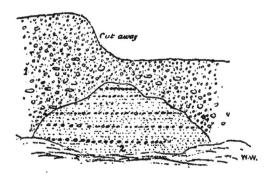

1. Gravel and sand. The gravel irregular, composed largely of flint pebbles,
   but also with pebbles of chalk ; partly coarse, and with large flints and
   other stones (Glacial Drift).
2. Sand, with layers of pebbly gravel, bedding flat, reaching up to about 8 feet
   above the bottom of the pit.

The sand-pit marked on the map, to the N.W., shows a different kind of
Glacial Drift.
Various pits in the Boulder Clay, west of Reydon, have been dug through
to the pebbly gravel (see p. 41).

Southward of the clay plateau the gravel extends down to the
marsh-level, and for the most part continues to do so thence eastward, Chillesford Clay cropping up at one place only (see p. 18)
and the Crag sand in two very narrow strips, together about 1½
miles long, chiefly up small side-valleys. It would seem therefore
that the series now described must be of considerable thickness
over at all events a large part of the tract between Wangford and
Easton Bavent.

A gravel-pit by the edge of the marsh nearly a mile and a quarter a little
E. of S. of Wangford church gave the following section, the divisions being
little else than varieties of one bed :—

Signs of more gravel above, from soil, &c.
Fine buff false-bedded sand, with loam in parts ; up to about 3 feet.
Light-coloured sand, partly loamy, with layers of gravel (chiefly flint-
    pebbles) ; about 3 feet.
Gravel, chiefly of flint-pebbles, most rather large ; up to 6 feet.
Light-coloured and ferruginous gravelly sand ; about 4 feet shown.

About a sixth of a mile eastward gravel and sand are to be seen, in a section on the southern side of the road, and there are other pits round about Reydon Hall* and Reydon Cottage.

South-westward of the latter place there are gravel-pits bordering the marsh, and it is probably here " in a pit close on the north-east edge of Reydon marshes" that Prof. Prestwich found (in 1869 ?) a layer " of the pebbly sand concreted by oxide of iron . . . . . full of the casts and impressions of *Mytilus edulis* in all stages of growth, and many of the shells double."†

Continuing our course along the northern side of the tidal tributary called the Buss Creek, which cuts off the Southwold Island, there are sections in sand and gravel, but one of which however is noteworthy. This is in a small pit two thirds of a mile N.N.W. of Southwold church, close to, and on the eastern side of, the road to Lowestoft. where, in some of the fallen masses of the pebble-gravel (with a layer of iron-sandstone) some impressions and casts of shells were seen, and a piece in place, with such impressions, was dug out. At a later visit, with Mr. W. M. Crowfoot and Mr. W. H. Dalton, actual shells were found in one corner, in sand at the bottom of the pit, the names of the shells found being given in the list at pp. 82–84.

Other sections, along the left bank of the Blyth, have been already noticed at pp. 14, 18.

### Southwold Island.

The town of Southwold, with its Common, is practically on an island, bounded on the east by the sea, on the south-west by the Blyth, and on the north-west by the Buss Creek, and only joined to the mainland on the north by the narrow strip of shingle that divides the Buss Creek from the sea. Our pebbly beds take up the surface of nearly all this island (except for the bordering marshes) newer beds occurring only at one part, and lower beds having been touched in only one section.

The cutting for the Railway Station was in pebbly gravel and sand, at the south up to about 7 feet deep. Here at the corner (under the hedge of the road), I found, about 5 feet down, a lenticular mass, six inches thick at the most, full of shells, which seemed to reach some 6 or 7 feet along the southern side, but less on the east. There was another very small shelly patch in a like position about 12 yards northward, on the eastern face. The fossils found here are named on pp. 82–84, partly from a list given me by Mr. W. M. Crowfoot, who visited the section with me afterwards and took away a mass of the shelly bed for examination.

The first cutting westward of the station is merely a short scrape, no more than 18 inches deep, in the gravel, and the next is only some 4 feet deep in gravel and sand.

The next at first is only up to 2½ feet deep and in the same bed, which is loamy in part ; but it then cuts through the higher part of the common, and, where the ground begins to rise, there is an irregular clayey layer in the gravel. The gravel contains beds and lenticular layers of sand, and before getting to the highest part a mass of sand, up to 5 feet thick, occurs in the midst. South-westward nearly all is gravel, sandy as usual and many of the pebbles being large. Only flint-pebbles were seen here. Probably shells occurred somewhere, as on the embankment of the branch to the harbour, a little away from where it leaves the main line, a lump of hardened sand and gravel with shells was found.

In the large old pit on the Common, marked as " Limekiln " on the old Ordnance Map, there is bedded pebble-gravel, with sand, and with one marked

---

* Unfortunately, on the old Ordnance map, this name is given to two places, and wrongly to the one here alluded to, about three quarters of a mile south-eastward from the church.

† *Quart. Journ. Geol. Soc.*, vol. xxvii., p. 462.

horizontal layer of large pebbles in the middle (shown at the western part). At the highest part (central) some of the beds in the upper part are loamy, and the layer of large pebbles (shown in a small pit within the larger one) is thicker. The eastern end and the southern side were overgrown.

There were no other noteworthy sections of the gravel when I lived at Southwold, except at part of the cliff, which will be described further on (p. 60), as well as the more important cliff-section of Easton Bavent, to the north.

### Easton Valley.

As before noticed, the pebbly beds are at the surface over the plateau between this valley and that of the Blyth below Reydon. Thence they crop out up the valley to Wangford, in part (near Reydon) reaching down to the marsh, and then down the left side, where, together with some overlying masses of Boulder Clay, they again form the plateau to Covehithe.

After leaving the Easton Bavent cliffs, noteworthy sections are scarce.

In an old pit on the northern side of the high road, nearly a mile north-eastward from Wangford, sand occurs beneath the Boulder Clay. Some of the sand is soft and fine, and would pass as Glacial; but some is sharp and gravelly, with a gravel layer, and contains broken shells (*Cardium*) at one place, so that it probably belongs to the Pebbly Series, though it is hard to say, the section being hidden.

To shew how slight variations occur in these pebbly beds, one may give an earlier section than that on p. 19, at the Frostenden brickyard. This was noted by the late MR. S. V. WOOD, Jun., who kindly sent me the following particulars :—

Coarse gravel, filling a hollow.

Bure Valley Beds.
{
Bright yellow sand, false-bedded in places -      - 5 feet.
Beach of pebbles, oblique, getting sandy at the base, and passing down into the next  } 6 to 7 feet.
Dark yellowish-brown sand [? 2 feet] -      -
}

Chillesford Clay.

A sand-pit on the western side of the high road, about a quarter of a mile S.E. of Frostenden Church, gave the following section :—

    Loam (? decomposed Boulder Clay), gravel, and sand.
    Light-coloured false-bedded sand, with irregular layers of pebbly
        gravel.

A sand-pit on the other side of the road, close by, above the junction with the lane running eastward, is in the lower bed of the above, here somewhat evenly and finely bedded (lower part), the gravel-layers regular, and, chiefly in the upper part, with a little fine false-bedding. In parts there is a little gravel at top.

The pit, marked on the map, on the northern side of Manor House, South Cove, gave the section below :—

    Fine, soft, bedded, partly clayey, buff and brown sand; up to about
        7 feet.
    Light-coloured and brown sharp gravelly sand; 1½ feet shown.

A like set of beds were again seen in a pit opposite the farm, about three quarters of a mile W. by S. from South Cove church, the details being as follows :—

    Gravelly soil, and pipes of gravel.
    Buff and brown fine soft sand, compact, bedded, partly loamy; up to
        about 9 feet.
    Sharp sand and gravel; about a foot seen.

### Covehithe and Benacre.

Around Covehithe the pebbly beds form the higher ground, with some capping of loam: but northwards, near Benacre, the Glacial Drift (sand and Boulder Clay) rises above them.

S.W. and W. of Covehithe, there is much sand; but gravel was seen over the Chillesford Clay W.S.W. of the church (see p. 20), and on the northern side of the road, about a quarter of a mile W.N.W. of the same, the clay was touched beneath gravel.

On the eastern side of the lane, nearly half a mile N.E. of the church, was a pit in sand, with a layer of gravel in the middle.

The beds shown in the cliff are described at pp. 72–75.

I am hardly satisfied with the mapping of the Benacre ground and do not pin my faith thereto; it is simply what seemed to me the most likely reading with the evidence at hand.

The broad spread of low ground eastward from the village is peculiar. It seems to be a flat of pebbly sand and gravel (? with Chillesford Clay near below), from above which rise, both east and west, sand-hills, those on the west clearly of Glacial sand, and the other probably so.

In the midst of the northern part of this flat tract, however, by the road through (and at the southern edge of) Church Cover, a small old shallow pit, mostly overgrown, showed, at one part, pebbly gravel over ferruginous sand (like Crag), which implies the absence of Chillesford Clay there. It seems possible, on the other hand, that this clay may occur along the northern edge of the wood, which is thickly overgrown.

It is hard to know how to end off the pebbly gravel north-west-ward. The gravel-flat north of what was the Walnut Tree Inn, is well-marked, and at a lower level than the Glacial sand, which forms a slight rise westward. But a like feature occurs further westward, between here and Henstead, and also N.W. of the latter place. In these parts, however, the gravel has more angular flints and a larger proportion of stones other than flints, and therefore it has been concluded, for the present at least, to class it as Glacial.

By the high road there was a small section, not far below the boundary of the Boulder Clay, of pebbly gravel over sand (like the usual junction of the pebbly gravel and the Crag); and in the hollow eastward there is damp springy ground, apparently from loam (? Chillesford), occurring below the gravel, etc.

Farther eastward, in the low ground bordering the marsh, northward of the church, there are more signs of the occurrence of this loam, whilst above the ground is gravelly.

It is possible that there are outcrops of our pebbly series higher up the valley, as indicated by the following sections, but if so they are probably inconsiderable in area, and without further evidence it would have been unsafe to map a further extension of these beds.

At the border of the marsh, more than half a mile northward of Henstead a small sand-pit at the eastern end of the little wood (in Sheet 67, S.) about a third of a mile W.S.W. of Rushmere Hall, 15 feet deep, but not clear, showed sandy and pebbly soil over light-coloured false-bedded sand, gravelly at the bottom, over light-coloured and bright-reddish brown sand, with loamy and gravelly layers (? Glacial beds over the pebbly sands).

The pit round the yard at the back of the cottages at the edge of the marsh about two-thirds of a mile N.W. of Henstead church shows irregular sandy gravel, mostly coarse, scooping into brown and buff more or less bedded sand with a pebbly layer in the lower part. This seems to be a junction of Glacial gravel with the pebbly sand. Judging from the dampness along the edge of the marsh westward the Chillesford Clay must be near the surface; however its outcrop is hidden, if only by a wash of sand.

*Note* to p. 25.

A remark by my colleague MR. C. REID that "the shingle at Westleton is now believed to belong to the Glacial Beds"* had been overlooked. As will be seen that belief has not been adopted by me, and the statement should have been qualified by the insertion of "by some observers," instead of having been made general.

* Memoirs of the Geological Survey. The Geology of the Country around Cromer, p. 9 (1882).

## CHAPTER 5. GLACIAL DRIFT.

### GENERAL REMARKS.

In our limited district the Glacial Drift may be described under two heads, the Boulder Clay and the beds between this and the Pebbly Series. This division it should be understood is adopted only as a matter of convenience, and without any prejudice to the general question of classification: for our local purposes it is not worth while to separate sundry small masses of loam and more or less sandy Boulder Clay from the far larger mass of sand and gravel, which seems to come between these and the still greater mass of the Boulder Clay.

There are, too, doubtful points. Thus, in the case of small isolated patches of Boulder Clay, it is sometimes impossible to say whether they belong to the great upper mass or to some local underlying bed; and it should be understood that Boulder Clay is by no means limited to one horizon in the Glacial Drift of East Anglia, but that comparatively thin layers occur locally in the beds beneath the thick wide-spreading sheet which takes up so large a part of the country. Again, Boulder Clay has a habit of weathering at the surface into a brown stony loam, the chalk being dissolved out by infiltrating water, and this resultant is so like some of the lower layers of sandy Boulder Clay or stony loam, as to be very deceptive.

### LOWER BEDS.

Under the above head are included sand, gravel, and occasional loam, which Mr. WOOD classed as Middle Glacial, and other loam and Boulder Clay belonging to his Lower Glacial. With small exceptions, too small indeed to be shown on the map (but for a patch S. of Dunwich) these beds are limited to the tract north of the Blyth.

The chief constituent is sand, which is marked, to a great extent, by being charged with grains of chalk, the dissolving out of which has been hindered by overlying Boulder Clay. Such chalk grains however seem not to occur in other sands, even when capped by Boulder Clay, and they may be taken as an evidence of Glacial age—in this district.

#### *South of the Blyth.*

The evidence for the little bit of Glacial sand shown seven eighths of a mile S. of the ruined church of Dunwich is given in the account of the cliff-section (p. 54).

The pit at the back (east) of Stone Cottage, about two miles south of Blythburgh church, gave the following section, but the beds were a good deal hidden by talus :—

> Pale Boulder Clay, full of small stones, resting almost evenly on the bed below: weathers irregularly into a brown soil : up to 7 feet or more.

Light-coloured sand, with thin layers of loam and grey clay; more clayey
at the base (throwing out water) = Glacial brickearth.
Light-coloured sand, up to 7 feet seen.

The pit just E. of Hunton Lodge (which place is itself in 50, N.E.) was in
great part overgrown, in 1879, and where not so, all but the top was mostly
hidden by talus, but the following succession was seen:—

Boulder Clay, 3 to 5 feet (? more elsewhere, in the part not clear).
Light-coloured sharp sand, with shingly gravel; mostly a thin layer of the
latter at the junction with the clay; about 6 feet (? under 3 in parts).
Light-coloured bedded sand, mostly fine, with some thin layers of grey
clay or loam (the former in the upper part): some fine false-bedding in
the lower part; about 9 feet seen.
More shingly sand seemed, at one spot, to occur about a foot lower; but
one could not be sure about it. At a later visit (1880), the section was
deeper, and about 20 feet of sand (in all) was seen between the Boulder
Clay, and the bottom of the pit.

Whether the uppermost sand belongs to the Glacial Drift, or to the Pebbly
Beds, and whether that next below is also Glacial or belongs to the Chillesford
Beds could not be established.

In other cases it is possible that there may be thin masses of Glacial sand
next beneath the Boulder Clay.

The small cutting on the railway westward from Blythburgh Station gave
evidence of the occurrence of a little Glacial Drift close to the bottom of the
valley. At the eastern end there were (on the southern side) some little
patches of Boulder Clay (with gravelly soil above), but I could not make
sure that these were in place. Then, westward, there is gravel and sand, with
traces of building-materials at top in places, and at one spot (the highest part
of the southern side) a thin film of Boulder Clay. Then there is gravel over
gravelly sand, or sand. Then yellow sand, capped only by a gravelly soil;
and then, at the hedge-corner on the southern side gravel comes on irregularly,
as in fig. 4, which represents a length of about 20 yards and a greatest height
of 12 feet. Beyond this is more gravel and sand, with some included pieces
of Boulder Clay; and Boulder Clay is shown in a hole between the line and
a cottage. As there is no room on the map to show this patch of Drift, one
was forced to mass it with the pebbly gravel. Some of the gravel may be
River Gravel: it contains some large sub-angular flints. The sand at the base
may be Crag. The little gravel above the sand at the highest part, close to
the church, is pebbly.

Fig. 4.

*Section in the Railway Cutting, Blythburgh.*

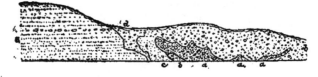

a. Chalky gravel in sandy Boulder Clay.
b. Sandy gravel.
c. Gravelly sand.
d. Gravel.
e. Sand, with a thin layer of gravel; with wash, to hedge, at top.

*Between the Blyth and the Easton Stream.*

The pits in the field N.N.W. of Bulchamp Farm (and two thirds of a mile
N.E. of Blythburgh) were ploughed over and hidden, except the southernmost

but one (near cottages) and this was turfed except at the southern end, where the section, fig. 5, was noted, after making some clearance with a spud. It was about 30 feet long, along a slight curve:—

Fig. 5.

*Section in a Pit near Bulchamp Farm* (1878).

Scale about 8 feet to an inch.

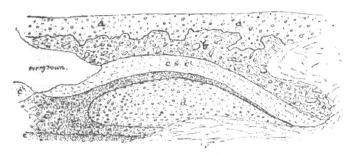

*a.* Sandy stony soil, piped and wedged into *b.*

<table>
<tr><td rowspan="8" style="writing-mode:vertical">Glacial Drift.</td><td>*b.* Pale Boulder Clay. At one spot at bottom only a stony loam. 3 feet or more, but partly turfed.</td></tr>
</table>

*b.* Pale Boulder Clay. At one spot at bottom only a stony loam. 3 feet or more, but partly turfed.
*c.* Sand, with loam, and stones (chiefly in one layer); up to a foot or more, but mostly less : passing into the next.
*c′.* Brown and grey bedded loam and sand, up to about 1½ feet.
*c″.* Boulder Clay, from 0 to a foot at the west; thickening east to about 4 feet suddenly, and wedging *under* the following.
*d.* Light-coloured sand and gravel (of flint-pebbles, chalk-pebbles, flints, some large, and large pieces of chalk) : up to about 4 feet, when the bottom foot is darker and loamy.
*e.* Chalky gravel, dug into to about a foot. Some Red Chalk in this and a bit of coal (?).

At about 20 feet from the eastern part some shelly Crag was seen at the same level as *e.*

From Uggeshall to Wangford there is a fairly broad outcrop of sand, between the Boulder Clay and the Pebbly Series, with a spot of loam on the road about half way. Naturally the boundary-line between this sandy mass and the sandy beds below is not of the most marked kind.

The pit at the back (north) of Manor House, Uggeshall, is overgrown, but must once have given a good section. At top there is clean clay, dark grey, weathering brown, which is mostly underlain by thin, fine, buff sand, and then there is buff Boulder Clay. The lower part is in light-coloured sand, with a gravel-layer, and at the base there is some ferruginous sand, also with pebbly gravel.

The sand-pit, marked on the map, a quarter of a mile E. of N. from Wangford church was mostly ploughed-over (1879), but the south-eastern side showed brown fine soft bedded sand ; and towards the entrance some buff sandy Boulder Clay seemed to abut against the sand, so that whether it was in or under the sand one could not tell.

At the wood, just north, there is an old pit in Boulder Clay, partly pale and sandy, cut through to sand, as far as could be seen.

A junction-section with the Pebbly Series, has been described at p. 28.

From the plateau of Reydon N.N.W. for about 1½ miles there is another outcrop of sand, with loam in places, which narrows in its course up the high ground of the Benacre Valley. In this case also the line between the Glacial beds and the underlying Pebbly Series is not always clear.

At Reydon Grange, at the old clay-pit (marked on the map), half a mile east of the church, and about three-eighths of a mile E. N. E. of the church three small patches of loam have been mapped, and a fourth at the following section.

The "Clay pit" (marked on the map) about half a mile north of Reydon church was mostly overgrown, and hardly used (1878). At the clearest part, north, light-coloured disturbed fine buff sand and gravel (of various stones) were shown to a depth of 12 feet, with fragments of shells in some of the gravel-layers (one large piece of *Cyprina Islandica*). In the middle of the pit, at the bottom, was a shallow cut showing a little gravel over buff laminated loam. At the eastern side there was Boulder Clay, mostly dark bluish-grey, the junction with the gravel being hidden; but the two beds must almost abut against each other.

A pit close by to the west, at the back (north) of the farm, showed gravel over loam.

The pit at the little wood, marked on the map, on the southern side of the lane a quarter of a mile N.E. of Reydon Hall is overgrown in the part marked as wood, but the southern part, in the field beyond, is in part clear, and the further southern end gave the section below, the beds being slightly waved.

Soil and traces of Boulder Clay, passing down into the bed below; up to 3 feet.

Glacial Drift.
- Buff laminated fine-grained sandy loam, passing down into the next; 4 to over 5 feet.
- Buff (paler) fine-grained soft compact sand, with loamy layers, and (generally, as far as can be seen) with a layer of coarse sharp sand and gravel, about 2 feet down, containing broken shells (*Cardium, Cyprina*? etc.). ? other like sand below, but the bottom not shown (? irregular layers); about 4 feet where most shown, and cannot be much more, as a lower cut, just by, continues the section thus :—
- Buff loam.
- Sand and gravel, with broken shells, about 2½ feet.
- Buff clayey loam.

In the triangular field between the lanes just north two small old ploughed-over pits show traces of Boulder Clay, which probably merely fills a hollow, as the ground above is sandy. The mapping here was difficult, the boundary of the Boulder Clay being indistinct.

## The Neighbourhood of Wrentham.

North of Frostenden the Glacial sand and gravel comes on in force, with a continuous outcrop (by Wrentham, Benacre, Henstead, Sotterly, and Ellough), and probably with a wide underground extension beneath the Boulder Clay. Indeed, it is possible that the outcrops of Uggeshall and Reydon may be connected underground with this mass, and of course the small isolated outcrop in the valley at Low Farm, Frostenden, is almost sure to be. It is doubtful, however, whether lower beds may not occur further westward from Benacre than is shown on the map (see p. 31).

Just N.E. of Frostenden church there is sand beneath the Boulder Clay, in a pit. An old pit, half a mile north of the church shows Boulder Clay over sand and gravel. Two old pits, more than half a mile and three quarters of a mile N.E. of the church, show Boulder Clay over gravel; whilst a third, on the eastern side of the road some three eighths of a mile E.N.E. from the church, again seems to show sand only, under the clay. These and the following two sections, all near together, show the variation from sand to gravel.

A little S.E. of the last-noted pit the line of old pit, westward from the back of the farm on the northern side of the high road about three quarters of a mile east of Frostenden Hall, was in great part overgrown in 1879, when the beds noted in the clearer parts were as below : —

> Brown stony loam, with Boulder Clay in parts (the loam is merely ⎫ Up
> weathered Boulder Clay); passes down into the bed below. ⎪ to
> Fine buff clayey sand. ⎬ 9 feet
> Light-coloured sharp gravelly sand. ⎭ seen.

There is water at the bottom, probably from Chillesford Clay being near.

Sand was again seen, under 6 feet of Boulder Clay, at the northern side of the road a quarter of a mile westward of Wrentham church.

In June 19, 21, 1880 the watercourse W.N.W. of Wrentham was mostly dry above the bend E. of Square Cover, but with some pools, the channel being in Boulder Clay. From that bend downwards, to just below the bridge N. of the church, the deeply-cut channel was quite dry, the bottom being in sand. The holes just below the bend are practically swallow-holes, whether natural or not.

The sides of the sand-pit, marked on the map, on the western side of the road, about a quarter of a mile northward of Wrentham church, are mostly hidden by talus; but at top, at the higher part, Boulder Clay, mostly weathered into brown stony loam, was seen, whilst below there is sand, partly gravelly, and like Glacial sand.

The northern part of the sand-pit, marked on the map, about half a mile E.N.E. of Wrentham church, was hidden in 1879; but the southern side was partly clear, and gave the section below :—

> Grey Boulder Clay, lying evenly on the bed beneath (as far as seen), the two being sometimes sharply divided, but sometimes less so; 2½ to 6 feet or more.
> Brown loam and clayey sand (the upper part more loamy, the rest more sandy), with a few stones, with signs of bedding, passing into the bed below (but the plane of colour-change marked); about 4 feet.
> Light-coloured sharp sand, seen to 6 feet deep; gravelly at the base.

Of course if the bed of loam continues far along the base of the Boulder Clay, it makes the boundary-line of the latter more doubtful, as it is not unlike the weathered Boulder Clay so general at the surface. This loam again is not unlike the stony loam that, in other parts, has been classed as Lower Glacial; and it may be a question whether the Sotterly brickearth (see p. 39), which is of a like character, is not, like this, merely a bed at the base of the Boulder Clay (or in the sands and gravels), instead of a lower division of the Glacial Drift.

In the ditch along a hedge, marked on the map, west of Wrentham Great Wood, and half a mile N.N.E. of the church, gravel is touched in places. Whether this is an uprise of the beds beneath the Boulder Clay, or a bed in the clay, cannot be told.

The clear part of the sand-pit, marked on the map, at Park Farm, about a mile east of Wrentham church, gave the following section, in 1879 :—

> Boulder Clay, the upper part darker and clayey, the bottom 2 feet or so pale and sandy; 3 to 5 feet.
> Sharp false-bedded sand, brown at the junction, the rest light-coloured, with white grains and with two gravelly beds; about 15 feet.

A shallow pit, in the north-eastern corner of a field, about a quarter of a mile S.W. again showed the junction, the pale Boulder Clay passing down into fine buff sand, loamy at the top. The Boulder Clay was for the greater part weathered to a brown loam, and most irregularly so, the loam sometimes going under the unweathered clay, and the junction with the sand was obscure, on the south, from this weathering.

Along the southern edge of the park at Benacre there are old overgrown pits, through Boulder Clay to sand. A large one, marked on the Ordnance Map, a quarter of a mile S.W. of The Hall Farm, showed some thickness of the clay on the north; but on the east, where it was ploughed over, sand seemed to come almost to the surface. Another large one (the most easterly of the set), just S.E. of the same farm, showed the junction at its south-eastern part, under the hedges engraved on the map, the bottom part of the clay having signs of bedding, the top part of the sand having interculated patches of Boulder Clay, and there being the usual white grains (? chalk) in the sand.

## Outliers, near the Coast.

Leaving the main mass for a time, some outliers, near the coast, may be noticed.

At Covehithe the Pebbly Series is sometimes capped by loam, as has been well seen in the cliff (see pp. 74–75). The patch about three eighths of a mile south-wards from the church is ill-defined, and has been limited (on the map) to the area of the old ploughed-over pits. In the larger mass eastward of the church there is a very large old pit, on the northern side of the road, cutting through the loam into sand. Although the section was hidden when I was there, and all that could be seen was some stony loam over sand, luckily it had been seen by the late Mr. S. V. Wood, Jun., some years before, and he was kind enough to send me a drawing, from which the following account is made :—

> Gravel, in part only, scooping into the beds below.
> Tawny loam, about 3 feet, passing down into the next.
> Loamy sand, about 4 feet.
> Loose yellow sand, 3 feet seen.

Mr. Wood classed the top bed as Middle Glacial, the next two beds as Lower Glacial, and the bottom bed with the Pebbly Series.

In the still larger outlier, chiefly of sand, eastward of Benacre, there is but one section; in the large old pit (with a barn in the middle) on the hill-top more than a mile E.S.E. of Benacre church, which was mostly ploughed over or overgrown, in 1878; but at the north-eastern part one could make out a capping of gravel (of subangular flints and pebbles), of loam with stones (? decomposed Boulder Clay), and at parts of a little Boulder Clay. Below, and elsewhere, sand only was seen, and this contained white grains.

In the field S. and S.E. of this there are old pits, with gravelly loamy and sandy earth at the ploughed-over sides, and at the northern edge of the mass, skirting the marsh, there is abundant evidence of the presence of sand.

## Benacre Valley.

Returning to the main mass we may now follow the outcrop up this valley.

The pit, marked on the map, about a sixth of a mile S.W. of Benacre church was much overgrown, but was clear at the south (1878), where the beds seen were :—

> Bluish-grey Boulder Clay, apparently in a slight scoop.
> Sand, the top 3 or 4 feet brown, and the uppermost 2 feet bedded (con-formally to the junction with, or rather the passage into, the clay), with clayey stony layers, some of the stones being hard glaciated chalk. In the middle part of the pit the sand dug was fine, false-bedded, pale buff and with white grains.

Two sections, northward and north-westward of Henstead, which may perhaps show a junction with the Pebbly Series, have already been noticed (pp. 31–32).

At Low Pasture Plantation, north-westward of Henstead church, the mapping is doubtful. There are traces of Boulder Clay in ditches in the low ground, and perhaps also the Chillesford Clay comes up higher than is shown on the map.

A small pit on the northern side of the lane, about a mile a little N. of W. from Henstead church (or a quarter of a mile S.W. of the Parsonage), showed at one part, buff loam with stones (? weathered Boulder Clay), filling a small hollow; the rest of the section being in buff bedded sand, with layers of gravel, pebbly, but not so much as in the pebble-gravel.

An old pit, by the barn about a quarter of a mile S.S.W., is in like sand, but not gravelly at the bottom.

At the head of the hollow in the Boulder Clay just N.E. of Woodrow Farm, and nearly a mile westward of Henstead, a pit showed loam over sand, whilst a neighbouring pit, about a quarter of a mile N.W. of the same farm, and also close to the boundary of the Boulder Clay, showed sand and gravel.

In the sand-pit marked on the map, on the eastern side of the tributary-valley, more than half a mile north of Sotterly church, pebbly gravel, the lower part with much sand; from 0 to about 7 feet thick; slightly scoops into the light-coloured sand (1880). This section, which is about 30 feet deep, and other pits eastward, remind one of the junction of the pebbly gravel with the Crag sand; but it can hardly be that we here meet with these beds; it would seem rather to be one of those repetitions that make the Drift so puzzling, and its classification so troublesome.

The large old overgrown pit, marked by an enclosure on the Ordnance Map, just N.E. of Sotterly church shows a little Boulder Clay, passing (or weathered) into a stony loam, from 3 to 4 feet thick, at the highest part, to some extent passing down into light-buff fine sand, which is cut into to 15 feet or more.

Sotterly brickyard, marked on the map, about three quarters of a mile S.W. of the church, gave the following section, in 1880 :—

> Boulder Clay. At one part light-grey above and dark-grey below, at another part all dark ; up to 8 feet thick and resting fairly evenly on the bed below.
> Brown stony loam, with signs of bedding; up to about 10 feet shown, at the western side, where, close by, there occurs beneath it :—
> Brown and grey sand. (See also well-section, p. 78.)

In a note, taken in 1868. Mr. E. T. Dowson records up to 15 feet of the loam, in which he found fragments of shells and a good sized boulder of sand-stone. Mr. C. Reid notes the occurrence of bivalve shells in this bed, which he calls Lower Boulder Clay. See, however, p. 37.

The late Mr. S. V. Wood, Jun., has referred to this section, as being in the "Contorted Drift" division of his Lower Glacial,[*] and as yielding traces of the species marked w. in the following list, the rest of which is on Mr. Reid's authority.

| | |
|---|---|
| ? Astarte borealis | Mactra ovalis. w. |
| Cardium edule | Pholas |
| Cyprina Islandica | Tellina balthica. w. |

Brown stony loam like that of the brickyard, with a little grey Boulder Clay above it, occurs in an old overgrown pit on the northern side of the lane about a quarter of a mile N.E.

A pit a little north of Willingham Hall (Ellough) showed sandy gravel over gravelly sand.


## BOULDER CLAY.

This, the uppermost part of the Glacial Drift in the district, is, in its unaltered state, a bluish-grey somewhat sandy clay, charged with a variety of stones, which consist chiefly of rounded and more or less scratched lumps of hard chalk and of flints, though contributions from Jurassic rocks are not uncommon, and older as well as newer formations are also represented. The stones are mostly of no great size, but some deserving the name of boulders occur.

By the infiltration of water two changes are brought about; the bluish colour is altered, by peroxidation of the iron, to a brown, and the chalk is more or less dissolved away, probably some of

---

* Quart. Journ. Geol. Soc., vol. xxxiii., p. 102.

the more clayey matter also going. The result of these changes
is a brown stony loam, which is sometimes so like part of the
lower Glacial beds that it is no easy matter to make out what
part of the Drift one is dealing with, where there is but a thin
mass that is almost wholly decalcified and altered. It is quite
possible therefore that some of the sections now to be described
are in lower beds, rather than in part of the great upper mass.

In cases where a thin layer of gravel or sand comes between
two masses of Boulder Clay it is possible that such sandy layer
may represent the Middle Glacial of MR. WOOD, and that the
underlying clay may belong to his Lower Glacial ; whilst, on the
other hand, the said sandy layer may be only a lenticular mass in
the Boulder Clay. These are some of the uncertainties that
beset the worker at Drift.

The tract where the Boulder Clay occurs in force is of a different
character from the rest of the district, being our only example of
a clay-country, a plateau mostly of arable land, with little in the
way of collected habitations. Only one church, that of Stoven,
is on Boulder Clay, and this close by the margin.

Many of the sections showing the junction with underlying beds
have already been described; but others are more conveniently
taken here.

The many patches south of the Blyth are not only, for the most
part, very small in area, but also very thin, as is proved by the
pits dug through the clay to the gravel or sand beneath, the chief
of which are shown on the map by spots, of the colour for the
lower beds, in the midst of that for the Boulder Clay. Most of
these pits are old and not noteworthy, except in the case of some
described above.

Whilst most of these patches are on the plateau, there are some at a lower
level, as on the right bank of the Dunwich valley opposite Jointure and Brick-
kiln Farms, at the latter of which the clay has been worked. Again on the
right bank of the Blyth nearly a mile and a quarter W.N.W. of Walberswick
church, where an old pit passes through stiff Boulder Clay to sand; whilst at
Blythburgh church the clay occurs bordering the marsh (see p. 34).

North of the Blyth too there are other isolated patches, a few at low levels.
As in some of these it is doubtful with what particular Boulder Clay we are
dealing, these may be treated of before taking the few noteworthy sections in
the main mass.

The patch a little west of Wangford church, which runs down to the marsh,
is probably Upper Boulder Clay, as a spur of the main mass runs down to the
same marsh-level a little further westward. There is a large old pit in this
patch.

At the farm about a third of a mile S.S.W. of Uggeshall church, in an old
pit (now a pond, with overgrown sides) marked as a wood on the map, there
are to be seen brown loam and clay (one layer dark-grey), and sand ; but no
order could be made out, nor can one be certain what the beds belong to.

In the fields, S.E. from the church there are three old pits, the nearer two
quite overgrown, the further ploughed over. These have probably been dug
for clay, and there is a trace of Boulder Clay at the middle one.

In the patch south of Reydon it is not unlikely that we have also beds
belonging to the lower division as well as to the Boulder Clay proper.

Loam was seen in an old pit at the western end.

The southern and only clear part of another old pit, in a field about a third
of a mile southward of the church, showed about 10 feet of brown stony loam,
the upper 6 feet or so with small irregular pipey masses of gravel, and here and

there (at or near the bottom) traces of pale Boulder Clay. At the north, by a hedge, there is some sand. Of course the stony loam is taken to be merely weathered Boulder Clay.

In the pit, marked on the map, on the western side of the road, three eighths of a mile S. E. of Reydon church, the beds are nearly horizontal, but slightly waved, and the section, which is about 15 feet at the deepest, is as follows, at the part farthest from the road, the rest being overgrown :—

Boulder Clay, with irregular pipey masses of sand, and sandy soil, up to 8 feet.
Gravel, with a little loam at top, up to 1½ feet } 2 feet at S.
Sand, with fine gravel, 0 to 1¼ feet
Buff sandy Boulder Clay, paler than that at top, about 5 feet.
Sand and gravel, dug into, at one spot to 3 feet.

At the north-west the two Boulder Clays nearly come together.

An old pit just south, in the next field, is overgrown, as also another (marked on the map) on the other side of, and touching, the road. This last seems to be in more sandy beds, but it held water at the bottom.

The south-eastern part only of the old pit in the field just south of Reydon Cottage was open in 1878, and this showed a few small pipes of gravelly earth over stony loam or clay, probably weathered Boulder Clay. An old ploughed-over pit a little to the west, by the hedge in the next field, seems to have been in sand and loam.

The following section was seen in a pit in a field about half a mile N.E. of Reydon church :—

Sandy and stony soil; up to 2 feet.
Bluish-grey Boulder Clay ; up to 2 feet.
Hard brown sand ; up to 1½ feet.
Buff bedded loam, some 3 feet shown.
? Sand beneath.

It is possible that the narrow strip skirting the northern side of the marsh of the Buss Creek, north of Southwold, may join underground (beneath the marsh) with the other strip which plunges down to the southern side of the same marsh at Southwold (see pp. 43, 60–62).

At the Southwold Railway Station there was some Boulder Clay lying about (in 1879), which Mr. J. P. Cooper, the Resident Engineer, told me came from the diggings for the foundations of the engine-shed. This clay may be a continuation of that to the east, at the brickyard and on the coast, and it must have ploughed sharply into the pebble-gravel. A hole 7 feet below the level of the rails was still in sand and gravel, and the well is said to have then passed through 13 feet of the like.

In the pit, marked on the map, on the northern side of the lane, a mile and a quarter N.N.W. of Reydon church, the Boulder Clay is underlain by chalky gravel.

In the largest outlier, at South Cove, there was an instructive section at the southern end, in the large clay-pit, marked on the map, a little southward of South Cove church, the eastern part only of which was clear in 1879. This apparently cuts across an old and shallower pit, for the top part looks as if it had been filled in to some extent. Buff and pale-grey sandy Boulder Clay, from 9 to 18 feet thick, rests irregularly on, and makes plunges into, sand. The clay is mostly bedded, the lower part particularly, with thin layers of fine buff sand, expanding in places to lenticular masses up to 2 feet in thickness. It weathers irregularly into a stony loam at the top; and still more, where the pit touches the road (at its south-eastern corner) this weathering may be called destructive, that is to say, there is nothing but stony loam, with signs of bedding. In one part the planes of bedding could be traced through stony loam and Boulder Clay alike, showing that the difference is merely one of condition.

On the other (southern) side of the road are traces of another pit, which has been ploughed over, as also has the pit, marked on the map, in a field to the south and around which are traces of Boulder Clay.

In the outlier to the S.E. there have been good sections, which, though much hidden in 1879, gave some information, as follows :—

The large old pit in the field about three quarters of a mile E.S.E. of South Cove church is mostly ploughed over, but great part of the northern side was not, at the time of my visit, and the clearer spots showed brown loam with stones, which, when not hidden by talus, was seen to pass down irregularly into light-coloured sandy Boulder Clay, with small stones, of which, however, little was exposed.

Near the above, and less than a mile from South Cove church, is another old pit in a field, which too is mostly ploughed over or overgrown. Where clear some 2 feet of soil, and a pipe of brown loam (with gravel-bottom) were seen above brown stony loam, 10 feet or more thick, with sand beneath, but hidden by talus. The stony loam shows bedding, and has some thin sandy layers, and it seems as if the sand rose to a higher level in other parts.

Turning now to the main mass, which forms the higher ground within an irregular boundary by Stoven, Uggeshall, Wangford, Reydon, Frostenden, Wrentham, Benacre, Henstead, Sotterly, and Ellough, plentiful signs of clay occur, though good sections are rare.

At Blomfield Brickyard, a mile east of Uggeshall church, there is bluish Boulder Clay, and at one part clean blue clay is said to be found about 10 feet down.

A pit, marked on the map, a mile west of Reydon church showed the following beds :— .

> Soil and buff Boulder Clay, partly decalcified to a pipey brown loam (as usual), 8 or 9 feet.
> Pebble-gravel and sand, about 6 feet shown.

A pit on the eastern side of the lane, about a mile S. of W. from Reydon church gave in part a clear section, as follows :—

Glacial Drift.
> Pale Boulder Clay, 5 to 8 feet or more ; the upper part irregularly decalcified to a brown loam with stones, and having the usual deceptive look of a later deposit in pipes in the clay.
> Light-coloured sand (where the junction is shown), ? from 0 to a few feet. ?=Middle Glacial of Wood.

Sandy pebble-gravel, 3 to 4 feet seen.

The pit on the other (western) side of the lane, and just south of the house, is overgrown; but the same beds were seen.

The pit on the opposite side of the lane to Red House, three quarters of a mile eastward of Wangford church, was in great part overgrown, but the north-eastern corner showed bluish-grey Boulder Clay, with, rising up from beneath, a hump consisting of sand with a clay-layer, some 6 inches thick, and then a yellowish loam. This sort of thing may occur in the fields to the west, at a rather higher level, the sand etc., perhaps coming up to the surface, and causing the sandy soil.

The pit at the back of Whitehouse Farm, about three quarters of a mile S.S.E. of Frostenden church, is much hidden by talus in the lower part, and the beds cut into are as follows :—

> Pale sandy Boulder Clay, 10 feet or more thick, with signs of bedding. Irregularly weathered at top by the dissolving out of the chalk-stones, to a brown stony loam ; the weathering in some parts clearly going across bedding-planes, which then run alike through loam and Boulder Clay.
> Light-coloured sand and gravel, 6 feet or more. Junction hidden.

By the northern edge of Benacre Park the junction of Boulder Clay with sand was seen at four places, between the section south-west of the church (p. 38) and the high road, and again in an old pit about a third of a mile west of the former Walnut Tree Inn.

The western wall of the new kitchen-garden (1880) at Sotterly Hall has its foundation in Boulder Clay down to the hollow E.S.E. of the house, by the roadway.

## CHAPTER 6. POST GLACIAL BEDS AND COAST CHANGES.

Of beds newer than the Boulder Clay there is but little in the district, save for the alluvial deposits of the streams ; and on the Boulder Clay plateau none of those gravels are found which in other parts of Suffolk, and in Norfolk, have been regarded either as early Post Glacial or as the latest member of the Glacial Drift.

### RIVER DRIFT.

Of the gravels and loams deposited by the rivers when they had a more torrential character than now, there are small, but in some cases fairly-marked, patches, all at low levels, and bordering the marshes.

In the Dunwich Valley there is a narrow gravelly strip, on the northern side, from about a mile and a quarter above the village downward for nearly a mile, and in the marshes north of the village there are small gravelly islands, rising a few feet above the marsh-level, the most southerly of which, N.E. of Bridge Farm, is hardly more than a mound of gravel and sand.

It is possible that the islands in Westwood Marshes may consist partly of Valley Gravel.

In the Blyth Valley the spur of Bulchamp Farm, below Blythburgh, ends on the south with a small gravel-flat, having a small pit, in gravel and sand, at its western side.

The only other occurrence in this valley is on Southwold Island, on the southern slope of the side-valley of the Buss Creek, where the Post Glacial beds follow the Boulder Clay that scoops into the Pebbly Series from the cliff for some little way inland.

The occurrence of brickearth here was noticed by PROF. PRESTWICH,[*] who has recorded the section laid open when the brickyard was close to the cliff, the pits then showing from 5 to 10 feet of brickearth and gravel, with remains of *Elephas primigenius*, over Boulder Clay. The following notes must refer also to this pit, and they show a greater depth of the deposit.

MR. VERTUE, of Southwold, told me, in 1879, that, some 12 years before, he got bones, about 15 feet down in clay, in a pit near the cliff, now ploughed over. The foreman at the brickyard stated that, at the lowest part here, close to the beach he had sunk 18 feet through the clay, to green (? wet) sand.

The bones were sent by MR. VERTUE to the College of Surgeons ; but no trace of them could be found there in 1879.

This pit (close to the beach) was reopened in 1880, when some irregular gravel was seen, filling pockets in, or rather splashed into, grey clay mottled brown.

Elsewhere there is clay with small chalk-stones (Boulder Clay) below the brick-clay, and the former rises towards the town.

In the Benacre Valley two small patches of Valley Gravel have been mapped, on either side. One of them is by the edge of the marsh north of Reydon Grove, where there was a small pit, in irregular sand and gravel. The other, nearly opposite, also faces the marsh. Here, a little southward of the Yarn Hill Pit, described above (p. 15) was a pit, about 10 feet deep, in irregular gravel, of flint-pebbles, subangular flints, etc., which had been worked further westward. From its position, and from its difference from any of the Glacial beds of the district, this was thought to be a Post Glacial River Gravel.

---

* *Quart. Journ. Geol. Soc.* vol. xxvii., p. 462.

On the lower ground of the Crag sand about a mile inland from Dunwich cliff there is a short low ridge, running S.W. and N.E. which seems to consist of blown sand.

## ALLUVIUM.

The deposits formed by the modern streams are of no great geologic interest, and are rarely seen in section. They consist mostly of fine-grained material, generally clayey, but sometimes with much sand, and layers of peat or peaty earth.

Where these deposits protrude beyond the beach, on the shore, the peaty layers, when they contain remains of trees and distinct traces of vegetation, are known as Submerged Forests, which have a large geologic literature. These occurrences are owing to the cutting-back of the coast, the consequent throwing-back of the beach, and the exposure, at low tide, of the freshwater deposit. I believe that nothing of the sort has been noticed in the case of the Blyth, the chief river of the district, probably from the shingle at its mouth, and along the marshes to the south, reaching to below low water-mark. Should this arrangement ever alter we shall hear of the discovery of another submerged forest, as the alluvium most certainly extends seaward for a little way beyond the shingle. In such places, and in no others, do these submerged forests occur.

At their western end, above the larger of the two islands of sand and gravel there, Westwood Marshes pass into a peculiar flat tract, sandy and, at the west, gravelly, boggy, with small fir-trees and in parts with gorse or heath. The boundary was therefore hard to draw, as, on the west the alluvium shades off into the sand-tract.

The ditches along the railway across the marshes about a third of a mile S.E. of Blythburgh church, cut peat or peaty earth, and those two thirds of a mile in the same direction from the church cut peaty earth and peat. A hump of sand is just touched at the wood (and road), the sand being blackish in great part.

The ditches by the side of the railway across the Southwold marsh, north of the Blyth, showed at first (nearest the land) peaty earth, and then, along the greater part of their course, the ordinary alluvial clay, at one part, near the river, rather finely bedded: it contained some freshwater shells.

At Easton Broad there can generally be seen peaty masses, consisting largely of more or less closely-packed stems or rootlets of some reed-like plant, cast up on the beach; and at extreme low tides some of this alluvial earth may, I believe, be seen below the beach.

This "submerged forest" has unfortunately been mistaken for the old Pre Glacial "Forest Bed,"[*] which is first seen, going northward, at Kessingland Cliff, and, to avoid such mistakes in future, it is well to note that this Easton deposit is really of very late Post Glacial age, merely the product of the present stream.

It does not run beneath the Chillesford Clay of the cliff, but is in a hollow cut out of that bed.

---

[*] J. GUNN. *Quart Journ. Geol. Soc.*, vol. xxiv., p. 462, and vol. xxvi., pp. 551, 555. Can the frontlet of *Cervus carnutorum*, referred to by PROF. DAWKINS, *Quart. Journ. Geol. Soc.* vol. xxviii., p. 409 (1872) and by Mr. E. T. NEWTON, *Geol. Mag.* dec. ii., vol. vii., p. 450. (1880) have come from this bed?

Its true character was noticed long ago by MR. S. V. WOOD, Junr., who said "the so-called Forest-bed at Easton Bavent is a post-glacial and very recent peat, occupying the valley-bottoms and occurring on the beach only in the places where the valleys open to the sea."[*]

Again, by the little Broad, south of Covehithe, this rootlet-alluvium, as it may be called, occurs below the shingle, on its seaward side; and by the hollow a little northward (see p. 73) alluvial mud, with rootlets, close to the land. By the southern end of the broad shingle-mass that bars Benacre Broad, peaty alluvium was seen in a like position, over three quarters of a mile E.N.E. of Covehithe church.

## COAST DEPOSITS.

Of the masses of shingle, piled up by the sea, sometimes in successive "fulls" or ridges, we have fair examples; but of hillocks of blown sand, carried up from the shore by the wind, there is little in the district. An inland occurrence of the latter sort has been already noticed (p. 44). Sand is indeed rare along this coast-line, whilst shingle-beach is ever present, in a long line, broken only by the Blyth (at rare times indeed not even by that stream) and sometimes opposite the Broads.

The first spread of old shingle, not now touched by the sea begins north of Dunwich, and runs to the Blyth, from the other side of which it continues to Southwold. This was described by MR. J. B. REDMAN, more than 20 years ago, as follows :—" For 4 miles in front of Dunwich Bay, the shore is 100 yards broad, consisting of 40 yards of old, grass-grown shingle next the marsh land, 100 yards of modern shingle, and 20 yards of sand foreshore to half-tide level . . . . . The shingle increases in breadth and height south of Southwold piers."[†] It will be seen from the map that the inland boundary of this shingle is irregular, and it is probably liable to change from the occasional carrying over of shingle by high seas.

The shingle at Southwold Harbour, the mouth of the Blyth, is ever shifting, and, whilst living at Southwold, I often noticed the movements.

At one time there was a fairly broad channel, at another the shingle was heaped across so as to leave but a mere cut through, at low water; but a continuous bar, damming the mouth of the river, was not seen, though I heard that one was occasionally formed; and MR. REDMAN (to continue quoting his paper, pp. 205, 206) says that "under certain conditions of wind, the mouth of the harbour is entirely choked with shingle, and has been inaccessible to shipping for weeks together. This was the case in 1859, so that persons could walk across the mouth of the harbour; and during the spring of 1860, the beach was driven across the entrance up to high-water mark by easterly winds. During the winter of the same year, the ferryman and others used to walk across the entrance for two or three weeks continuously . . . . . . . The land-water accumulating behind was frozen over, so that the harbour was literally sealed up within and without." Such an occurrence was afterwards recorded, in the *Times* of 26 March 1883, in a letter signed JOHN ATTFIELD, which says, "That is the present condition of the Blyth . . . . . . The easterly gale of the last two days has so lashed the waves on that coast that banks of shingle three yards thick, a score or two wide, and hundreds long, may be seen between Southwold and . . . . . . Dunwich." [As above noted there is always shingle there !] "One

---

[*] In a note to his father's paper, *Quart. Journ. Geol. Soc.*, vol. xxii. p. 547 (1866).
[†] *Proc. Inst. Civ. Eng.*, vol. xxiii., p. 205 (1865).

such closed the Blyth the night before last. I walked across the mouth myself, dryshod, on this Good Friday."

Again quoting MR. REDMAN's paper, which is a mine of information on our East Coast, "The early condition of the shore is plainly shown by a drawing . . . . . in the Cotton Collection, A.D. 1509–47,—when two arms of the sea flowed over Westwood Marshes at the back of Dunwich." [Strangely enough Dingle Marshes seem to be ignored in this rude map], "and over Reydon Marshes and Buss Creek at the back of Southwold, with a common outlet at Walberswyck Gatway, which appeared at that time to have a fathom and a half of water under favourable conditions. The estuary was, however, even then liable to be choked up. This took place as early as 1328, by the N. and N.E. winds prevailing, and the pent-up waters burst a new outlet, 2 miles farther north, which must have been at the end of Buss Creek" (p. 206). He then describes later changes, chiefly brought about by artificial means, and notices the beach north of the Blyth as "70 yards in breadth, from the sea-wall in front of the Town Marshes, the earlier 'fulls' being overgrown" (p. 207).

The next mass of shingle, inland from the actual beach, is that which bars the Buss Creek, and forms the only connection of what would otherwise be the Island of Southwold with the mainland.

At Easton Broad the shingle-bar that divides the lake from the sea is liable to being broken through. Direct communication between the inland water and the sea is then set up, and, as the tide falls, there is a very strong flow out through the narrow channel. I noticed that, on such an occasion, the sandy shore of the lake, at the foot of the shingle, was much covered by jelly-fish, left by the falling tide, whose bodies soon dried up to a mere film. I did not see a like breach made at the little Broad to the north; but this most likely happens.

At Benacre Broad, in front of which is a broad mass of shingle, a very high tide that occurred before my first visit (1878) had caused an overflow of sea-water over great part of the marsh, which killed the fish of the Broad in great numbers, and afterwards produced a singular effect along the border of the marsh, all the bushes being killed by the salt water, so as to produce a line of dead vegetation skirting the marsh, in striking contrast to the verdant growth that immediately succeeded.

The wide mass of shingle, partly covered with blown sand on the north, that fronts Benacre Broad, stretches northward, from the northern end of Covehithe Cliff, for 1¾ miles, to Sea Row (Kessingland), barring the Benacre Valley, the water of which runs through the channel cut through the shingle and known as Benacre Sluice. Along the part fronting the higher ground, between the two sets of marshes, the width of this shingle, measured on the new Ordnance map, varies from 1,200 feet, near the south, to about 850 on the north, not counting the part between ordinary high and low water, which would add some 40 feet, or more.

The difference between the old map and the new is noteworthy. On the former the most easterly point of the shingle is about due east of the southernmost point of the Broad; on the latter it is 1½ miles further north, a position which, I believe, it had not quite reached when seen in 1879. The difference is due of course to movement of beach.

Of this beach-spread MR. REDMAN remarks that it is "formed of sea-sand, now (1863 or earlier) covered with gorze and fine turf over the entire surface. Three distinct ancient mounds of shingle may be traced. A walking-cane pushed through the heather and rich mossy turf grates immediately upon the beach. Seaward there is a considerable area of sand-hills, and then a high mole of modern shingle, the sand-hills being separated from the ancient and modern shingle belts by two broad and deep parallel valleys. South of Benacre Sluice, the following are the widths :—

200 yards ancient shingle in several parallel belts;
150 „ sand-hills 30 feet high;
30 „ upper 'fulls' of modern shingle, 10 feet above high water; ·
60 „ shingle and sand foreshore to half-tide range.

or 440 yards in all south of Kessingland."*

---

* *Proc. Inst. C.E.*, vol. **xxxiii.** p. 208.

Presuming that the above is a maximum measurement, yet it exceeds the present maximum.

Between the "New Cut," which carries the water from the valley of Benacre Broad northward, by the western edge of the shingle, to a drain communicating with Benacre Sluice, and the hedge running roughly parallel with that cut, on the west, Blown Sand is banked up against the rising ground. This sand is divided into two strips, by the little hollow at Beach Farm, and in each strip there is a slight incurving at the ends, except at the far north. In no other part could one map the Blown Sand separately from the shingle.

## WASTE OF THE COAST.

### *General Remarks.*

The district is noted for the loss of land that has occurred along its sea-margin. According to old histories and traditions Dunwich was once a large town, with many churches, of which now two only remain, one in ruins and little more than 40 feet from the edge of the cliff, whilst the place is now a small village: again Covehithe Cliffs are said to have once jutted out so far that they formed the easternmost point of England, instead of Lowestoft doing so. It is not proposed, however, to go into this part of the subject; but rather to refer to what has happened in later times, and is happening now.

In the first place whilst the cutting-back of the cliffs still continues on the north, especially at Covehithe, on the south there is little change. This is accounted for by the protection of the base of the cliffs at Southwold, and by the accumulation of shingle which forms a natural defence. At Dunwich this state of things seems to have held for years, the base of the cliff being hidden by a slope of fallen earth, which is not carried away by the sea, or at least is rarely touched. At Easton Bavent, Covehithe, and Kessingland, on the other hand, the base of the cliffs is within reach of high tide, and consequently fallen earth is swept away.

Very generally these "incursions of the sea," as they are called, are put down as wholly owing to the action of the sea: it will be well to get rid of this notion, and to point out what really takes place.

It will be found that cliffs in such comparatively soft materials as we are dealing with, sand, gravel, and clay, rarely approach the perpendicular, but form a slope, generally of an uneven kind. On examining the processes of destruction it will be seen that these do not begin by an undermining of the base of the cliff, by the sea; but by the sliding down of masses of earth from the top. These earth-falls are caused by actions from above, by cracks formed by frost and by the drying of clay by the sun's heat, by rain, and sometimes by the blowing away of loose sand beds. The sea does little else than carry away the broken up material thus brought down to the cliff-foot, leaving the way clear again for further falls. At Covehithe certainly, where the cliff is low and its destruction rapid, there is little talus; it has no time to accumulate, and so the cliff is more abrupt. Of course were it not for the action of the sea in carrying away the loose fallen matter, the cliffs would soon weather to a slope, would become overgrown, and would then stand.

Nature therefore teaches us how to guide and to moderate her actions. Encouragement for the accumulation of shingle, and the conversion of cliffs into slopes, with guarded bases, seem to be the two works essential for stopping the loss of land along such a coast as that of Suffolk, a coast formed of easily moved materials. The taking away of shingle, or of sand, from a beach is of course a thing that should not be allowed: shingle taken away at one place, where it may be plentiful, may have a serious effect on another place, to which otherwise some of it might be carried naturally.

### Dunwich.

On September 24th, 1880, the following measurements were made at and near the ruined church on Dunwich cliff:—

From the northern buttress of the chancel to the nearest part of the edge of the cliff, about 43 feet.

From the edge of the cliff, along the southern hedge of the churchyard, to the Priory wall, about 112 yards.

Footpath south of the church (Temple Hill); from where it comes out of the wood to the edge of the cliff, 40 yards.

By a strange chance, whilst staying at the inn at Dunwich, at the time when the above measurements were taken, a reference was found to a measurement given in Gardner's book,[*] as having been made on September 26th, 1772, or almost exactly 108 years before, "from the cliff to the east end of the chancell" (of All Saints Church, now ruined) 70 yards. This is the same starting-point as the first of the measurements above, and it shows therefore that in 108 years the loss, at this spot, has been 167 (210–43) feet, or at the rate of about 18¼ inches a year. As the present rate seems to be much less, (indeed there was little waste during my stay in the neighbourhood), we may judge that some years ago the waste was at a greater rate. This conclusion is borne out by the fact that the old Ordnance Map fairly represents the present position of the coast-line, showing that there can have been but little change for many years.

### [Southwold.

Whilst living here no change could be noted, the low cliff being fairly protected. Mr. REDMAN, however, says that "this place suffered much during the winter gale of 1862. Large portions of the cliff were then washed down, and this was no doubt induced by the constant degradation of the cliff south of Covehithe Ness."[†] This degradation, however, still continues, as will be seen.

---

[*] THOS. GARDNER. Historical Account of Dunwich, 1754.
[†] Proc. Inst. Civ. Eng., vol. xxxiii. p. 207.

## Easton Bavent.

In 1841 CAPTAIN ALEXANDER communicated to the Geological Society some measurements of the loss of land here, which are worth reproducing.

"From careful observations, made during the last five years, Captain Alexander is of opinion, that the local statements, of 350 yards in breadth having been destroyed at Easton Cliff in about thirty-five years, are not much overrated, as, during that period, a nearly square field, containing twelve and a half acres, has been entirely removed by the sea, and as only three acres remain of another which consisted of eighteen and a half. This ratio of loss, he says, has extended along the whole range of the cliff except at the extreme south end. During the five years . . . . . the annual loss in breadth has been at least seven yards."[*]

In 1878, a marked change had taken place in this cliff since the date of the old Ordnance Map, the loss varying from a little at the southern end (as noticed by CAPTAIN ALEXANDER in 1841) to over a twentieth of an inch (on the scale of an inch to a mile) in the central and northern parts. Both at Easton and at Cove-hithe the Geological Survey Map has been altered, to fit the condition of things seen in 1878. The new large scale Ordnance Maps being now published, it will be a simple matter in future to measure the loss that takes place.

Unfortunately I omitted to record the figures of a measurement which would have enabled me to tie on my older records to that now given us.

Mr. REDMAN (in a footnote dated 10th July 1865) tells us that "the edge of the cliff is now 14 yards from the east angle of the farm buildings at Easton Bavent."[†] At my first visit to this cliff it had been cut back so far that some of those buildings had gone.

My first measurement was taken on October 31st, 1878, when the fine barn (now gone) was some way from the edge of the cliff, which was then over 20 feet beyond the eastern corner of a hedge that existed a little in advance of the barn.

On June 24th, 1879, the cliff had been cut back just to this corner, or about 20 feet in 8 months, and on July 7th the corner had been much cut off, the north-eastern corner of the barn (that nearest the sea) being then about 30 feet from the cliff, and the north corner 47½ feet.

On May 7th, 1882, the barn had been almost wholly destroyed, only a bit of wall being left.

On the new Ordnance Map no part of the barn is shown.

PROF. JUDD tells me that, on July 26th, 1884, the south-eastern corner (that nearest the sea) of a barn was 90 paces from the edge of the cliff, or probably about 230 feet. This measurement would seem to refer to the barn inland from the farm, which is shown as about that distance from the cliff on the new Ordnance Map.

We are indebted to my former colleague, Mr. F. DREW, of Eton College, for the following measurements, which he was kind enough to make whilst at Southwold on August 12th, 1886 :—

1. From the corner of the present shed to the cliff, 98 paces of 33 inches (about 270 feet) along the track, which is oblique to the cliff.

2. From the nearest corner of the last pulled-down building, next to that shed, to the cliff, 78 paces (about 215 feet) along the track; or in a direct line 65 paces (about 179 feet).

If the first measurement refers to the most easterly point of the building shown on the new Ordnance Map, it would show a loss of 30 feet since that

---

[*] *Proc. Geol. Soc.*, vol. iii., no. 79, pp. 445,446·
[†] *Proc. Inst. Civ. Eng.*, vol. xxxiii., p. 207.

map was made. If, however, the second measurement refers to that point, as seems likely from PROF. JUDD's note, then the loss has been about 50 feet.

On the next rising ground, three eighths of a mile to the north, the distance to the cliff-edge, along the hedge running N.N.E. to the cliff, from where it is joined by the hedge running N., was about 130 feet in May 1882, which is about the position shown on the new map.

My friend MR. H. H. FRENCH, who visited Southwold in the summer of 1887, was kind enough to take notes and to make measurements along the coast north of that town, which I am glad to be enabled to use in this Memoir. He concluded that from a spot about 50 yards south of the ruined farm north-wards to the end of these cliffs, little waste has occurred for some time, as, wherever the cliffs were high enough to give rise to talus, this was well-covered with vegetation, which would hardly be the case if the cliff were giving way. On the other hand the southern end of the cliff (from the spot 50 yards south of the farm) was without vegetation, the talus seemed freshly fallen and the cliff-face freshly cut; so that here waste has probably occurred of late.


## Covehithe.

In this case my measurements can be referred to the new Ordnance Map, although, in one place, the starting-point has been lost for some years, by the cutting back of the cliff.

At the southern end there has been little change. No exact measurement was made; but the low cliff-edge was close to the meeting-point of the two hedges or banks at the north-eastern corner of Green Heath, in 1878, as well as in June 1879, and that corner is shown as but little cut off, on the new six-inch map. In August 1887 MR. FRENCH measured the distance between these two hedge-banks, and found it about 70 yards, showing that there must have been much loss of land of late years.

Southward of the Coastguard Station, however, the edge of the cliff, in the summer of 1878, was at about the place where low water of ordinary tides is now marked, the corner, once formed by the meeting of the two hedges here, being then but little cut off. The new map shows, therefore, a loss of about 150 feet. In 1887 MR. FRENCH found the distance between the two hedges to be about 175 yards, again proving much loss.

Eastward of the Coastguard Station the distances to the cliff-edge along the lane were measured, at various times, starting at first from the point where the hedge on the north met that road, a point since destroyed.

In August 1878 it was about 100 feet from that point, along the northern side of the lane, to the cliff, or but very little inside where low water of ordinary tides is shewn on the new map.

On June 28, 1879, this distance had decreased to 80 feet, or a loss of 20 feet in about 10 months.

On June 23, 1880, a further decrease to 20 feet had taken place, or a loss of 60 feet in a year.

On May 7, 1882, the starting-point had gone; but, on the last occasion, the precaution had been taken of measuring back from this to the next hedge, joining the lane on its southern side, east of the Coastguard Station (about 350 feet) and now, measuring from this hedge, the distance to the cliff, along the southern side of the lane, was found to be about 320 feet (about where it is marked on the new map) showing a further loss of about 50 feet in 22½ months.

From August 1878, therefore, to May 1882 there has been a loss here of 130 feet. As the lane is not at right angles to the line of the cliff, though not far from it, some little deduction should be made. This may be done by adding three months to the time of observation, and thus putting the loss at 130 feet in four years, or at the rate of about 32 feet in a year.

Since the above was written, MR. FRENCH has sent me some measurements which he was good enough to take here in August 1887, with a tape a chain long. At that time the distance from the hedge to the cliff had decreased to 278 feet, a further loss of 42 feet in 5¼ years, or, allowing for the slight obliquity of measurement, less than 8 feet a year.

Taking the whole set of measurements, from August 1878 to August 1887, we chronicle a loss of 172 feet, or at the rate of a little over 19 feet a year, or say between 18 and 19 feet, to allow for the lane not being quite at right angles to the line of the cliff.

Of course the gradual cutting-back of the coast has an effect on the cliff-sections, things seen at one time being lost afterwards, and others not seen before, being shown, as will be noticed in the next chapter.

# CHAPTER 7.   CLIFF-SECTIONS.

## GENERAL REMARKS.

IT has been thought better to treat each of these sections as a whole, rather than to separate the various parts, making the description an explanation of the plate, on which the observed facts are shown.

The sections have been engraved to a horizontal scale of a foot to a mile, or an inch to 440 feet, and to a vertical scale $5\frac{1}{2}$ times as great (an inch to 80 feet), as without vertical exaggeration all the divisions could not be clearly shown.   Three points of detail are separately shown on a larger scale.

The measurements are, of course, not absolutely accurate.   The distances had to be got by pacing, with reference to fixed marks on the top of the cliffs as far as possible.   Absolute accuracy in this matter is not, however, important, as the sections change from time to time: indeed, many changes were noted whilst repeatedly examining the cliffs : it is enough to give a detailed representation of the facts observed during the years 1878–1880, when the Geological Survey of the district was in progress, some points having been noted at one time, others later.

The Plate is simply a reduction, carefully made by MR. J. G. GOODCHILD, of my sections, which were drawn in face of the cliffs, on the scale of two feet to a mile horizontally, and 40 feet to an inch vertically, that is twice the scales of the plate.

## DUNWICH.

### (LINES 1 AND 2 OF THE PLATE.)

This line of cliff extends for nearly two miles, from the northern edge of the marsh of Minsmere Level (in Sheet 49 S.) to about a quarter of a mile north of the ruined church of Dunwich, and contains the highest cliff of the district.

Owing to *talus* the base of the cliff was very rarely seen, and the only indication of the presence of fossiliferous Crag was the occurrence, on the foreshore at the southern end, of pieces of iron-sandstone with impressions of shells.   Earlier observers however, have been fortunate enough to see shelly Crag in place, and, before describing the section as seen by me, MR. E. T. DOWSON's note may be reproduced.

"In 1871 the attention of MR. W. M. CROWFOOT and himself was called to a shell-bed exposed in the cliff at Dunwich. This bed, a red crag, appeared in patches at the foot of the cliff, about 1500 yards south of the church-in-ruins, and it extended about 100 yards further south. Gradually rising from the beach level to a thickness of about three or four feet, it then disappeared at this level again. The general section of the cliff was as follows :—

> Light-coloured sand with veins of clay, about 30 feet.
> Unfossiliferous red sand, 3 to 7 feet.
> Shell bed. [A letter from MR. DOWSON describes this as red sand and shells.]

"The shells found here were, for the most part, of a fragmentary character, but in 1872 he obtained many perfect specimens in an exposure between tide-marks in front of the crag-bed shown in the cliff. Mammalian remains were also found, and these appeared to come from a hard ferruginous bed of clay and sand, shown here and there on the beach, some feet below the shell-bed in the cliff. At about 500 yards north of this spot, casts of shells appeared in the ferruginous bed."*

The names of the fossils recorded have been included in the list, pp. 82–84.

### Description of the Section as seen in 1878–80.

At the southern end sand only was seen, and this sand has throughout been classed as Crag, for reasons given at p. 6, and in this I differ from previous observers.

As the ground rises a thin layer of gravel, (chiefly subangular flints) is seen to occur, succeeded by more sand, and the succession is as follows :—

> Sand, with a few small stones, bits of clay, clay layers, and bits of shell.
> Layer of gravel at base.
> Sand, with very few small stones here and there in the top part.

Whether the upper sand should be classed with the lower may be doubtful ; but inland, where sections are few, it would be practically impossible to separate them.

Before reaching the highest part of the cliff the Pebbly Series comes on above, abruptly cutting into the sand at first, and then irregularly sinking to a lower level northward, where its base was hidden for a long way. At first, by the flagstaff, this bed consists of gravel at the top and of bedded sand with layers of gravel below. Then, at the highest part of the cliff, it is gravel ; then, as the ground falls northward, gravel and sand ; then, along the low ground, sand with gravel ; then, gravelly sand, with gravel at the base ; and then, before getting to the highest point of the rise, gravel at top, and sand and gravel below.

About 660 yards from the starting point the sand below was again seen, with the layer of gravel, but was lost directly, under talus, again to appear, rising up to the surface by the gully, some 800 yards from the beginning of the cliff. The Pebbly Series ends off as gravel, with patches of sand.

At the gully, which was cut down nearly to the foot of the cliff, the following section was noted :—

> Gravelly and peaty soil.
> Nearly white sand, with a thin layer of grey loam, a few small stones, and a layer of these at the base.
> Whitish sand, to the bottom of the cliff.

For some way northward only the sands were seen, covered with a gravelly soil in the hollow, the deepest part of which cuts through the persistent, though very thin, layer of subangular gravel.

About 630 yards north of the gully there is a small hollow of stony loam, with a gravel base in the lower part. This stony loam may be weathered Boulder Clay, or the result of the destruction of that clay.

Some 45 yards beyond this hollow the Pebbly Gravel again sets in, over the sand, to be itself cut into by loam, a thin mass of which last then occurs along

---

* *Proc. Norwich Geol. Soc.*, pt. iii. pp. 80, 81 (1879).

the cliff-top for some way. This stony loam is, probably, little else than weathered Boulder Clay.

Some 770 yards from the gully, at the base of the thin pebbly gravel, there comes in a little false-bedded sand, with broken clayey layers, and with gravel at the base at first. At nearly the same place there is, between the stony loam and the thin pebbly series, a lenticular mass of other beds, which it seemed to me might be thin representatives of Glacial sand and loam (? Middle and Lower Glacial of WOOD).

This mass extends to about 870 yards from the gully, and consists at first of bedded sand, from beneath which, northward, laminated clayey beds rise up, the section then being :—

> Stony loam and sand (? decomposed Boulder Clay); up to about 7 feet.
> Laminated grey and brown clay and loam; a layer of sand, with small stones, near the base; up to about 4 feet.
> Pebbly gravel, with layers of loam and sand; up to about 2½ feet, almost thinning out at the end of the hollow.
> White sand with the usual stony layer a few feet down.

Beyond this the stony loam, at the top, is a little thicker, cutting down to the whitish sand; but sometimes there is firm sand and sometimes a trace of clay and of gravel at its base.

At about 970 yards from the gully the pebbly gravel again sets in, and extends for a good way north, though but very thin, sometimes only 6 inches thick, and, at one spot, with black sand at the base.

At the same place there comes in, between the pebbly gravel and the stony loam (which suddenly cuts it off on the south) a thin bed of sand, most likely the same as that a little to the south, and sometimes, like this, with loam at the base.

At the spot marked A the details are as in Fig. A of the Plate. The thin clayey bed at the base of the upper (Glacial) sand extends north, and causes a line of damp.

A little further, where the stony loam ends off, about 1,060 yards south of the southern edge of the churchyard that is cut through by the cliff, the following were the details of the section :—

> Soil, nearly 2 feet.
> Brown firm sand, the upper part loamy, about 4 feet.
> Orange-coloured and grey clay, 6 inches.
> Fine pebbly gravel, the upper part with a matrix of coarse sand (as is also the case to the north), 1½ feet.
> White sand with a gravelly layer over 6 feet down; but no break traceable in the sand, only a colour-change some way lower.

Some 40 or 50 yards further the stony loam comes on again at the top, and, after awhile, cuts off the underlying sand, and then rests on the pebbly gravel, the two ending off near together, about 800 yards south of the churchyard, by the rise of the sand beneath. Before this happens, however, through there being less talus, the lower sands are more shown, and sometimes the lowest part seen is ferruginous and like decalcified Crag.

At about 850 yards from the churchyard the section is as follows :—

> Soil and Boulder Clay, the latter weathering to a stony loam, and passing down into sand; about 4½ feet.
> Sand, with gravel at the base (Pebbly Series); 1½ feet.
> Light-coloured sands, with a thin gravelly layer some 6 feet down, the sand for 2 feet below also containing some stones, and, at one spot, a patch of shells (too friable for extraction).

The particular interest of the section here lies not only in the occurrence of the shells, which it was impossible to identify; but also in the presence of Boulder Clay, in such a way as to lead to the conviction that the stony loam is merely that bed weathered.

About 80 yards further north there is a patch of Boulder Clay resting in a hollow in the sand.

At about 720 yards from the churchyard the gravelly layer in the sands rises up to the surface, and it was not noticed again to the north. All that is then seen is sand, the lower part of which is ferruginous and like Crag. The sand occurs, uncapped by anything but soil, until about 430 yards from the churchyard, where thin pebbly gravel again comes on; but for some way before this the soil is deeper and with bits of gravel at the bottom.

The sand here is of a deep orange-colour in the lower part; but change of colour is no reason for making a division.

The thin capping of pebbly gravel last alluded to reaches only for about 80 yards, being then cut off by a mass of washed-down material, that fills up a hollow in the sand, east of Grey Friars.

On the northern rise of the hollow here and just beyond the small earthwork (ditch) that is cut through by the cliff, the following section was noted :—

> Sandy wash, with stones, more or less bedded.
> Blown sand? black at top (? old soil),
> Layer of Gravel (base of the valley-deposit).
> Sand.

Directly the mass of wash ends the pebbly gravel comes on again in force, over the rising ground to the church; and, at the hedged footpath that runs, at nearly right angles from the cliff, through Greyfriars Wood, a small patch of Boulder Clay comes in between the soil and the gravel.

The base of the gravel, from here to within 50 yards of the churchyard-hedge, is finely bedded, with layers of buff clay, partly broken up (sometimes indeed with pebbles of clay). This clayey mass, at first very thin, increases northward to a thickness of 6 feet, and is in great part a distinct bed, of brown and grey clay, ferruginous, laminated, with sand, and often with pebbles; so that it is not quite like Chillesford Clay (which might be expected to occur in this position); but is suggestive of that clay having been worked up into the base of the gravel. Possibly when the coast extended much further out to sea Chillesford Beds may have occurred in the cliff, or perhaps they will be seen when the section has been cut much farther back.

At the spot marked B the section of this part was as follows (see fig. B of the Plate):—

> Bedded pebble-gravel, with clay.
> Lenticular mass of the laminated sand, clay, and ironstone about 8 feet
>     long and 22 inches deep. The crumpled bedding highly inclined, and
>     the mass clearly a detached block.
> Laminated clay, partly broken up, with sand and ironstone.

Just as this clayey mass ends off, at the base of the pebble-beds, Boulder Clay comes on above them, some 40 yards south of the churchyard-hedge, and continues, along the highest part of the cliff, for some 180 yards, when it may be seen distinctly, overlying the pebbly gravel. This clay is mostly covered by sandy soil, except north of the churchyard, and has partly weathered to a brown loam.

Just south of the churchyard the details of the section were thus:—

> Soil and blown sand, 6 feet.
> Boulder Clay, 4 feet.
> Pebbly gravel,? 14 feet.
> Sand.

In the middle of the churchyard thus:—

> Churchyard soil, 3½ feet.
> Loam and Boulder Clay, 4½ feet.
> Pebbly Series { Pebbly gravel, 4½ feet.
>               { Sand, with pebbles at the base, 3½ feet.
> Sand.

North of the churchyard the Boulder Clay has cut deeply into the gravel, the latter at one place being only 6 inches thick, whilst the base of the former is about 10 feet from the surface; and at last the gravel is cut off altogether, the Boulder Clay then resting on the sand beneath.

The cliff was then hidden, right up to the top, for some way, until, at nearly 140 yards from the churchyard, there was again a slight clearance, and the following section was seen :—

Gravelly soil and loamy sand.
Grey and brown clayey layer } about 1½ feet.
Gravel layer, chiefly pebbles
Sharp sand.

The little hollow, to the north, cuts through the Pebbly Series to bright ferruginous sand (seen to some depth beneath, where the footpath from the village reaches the cliff). The former, however, again comes on, just beyond the footpath, and caps the sand along the rest of the cliff, till the ground falls sharply beyond the flagstaff. The earth above the thin gravel is loamy; so that, possibly, some decomposed Boulder Clay may be present.

### Notes of other Descriptions.

The descriptions by other observers must now be noticed, and our great differences pointed out. Before taking up this part of the subject, however, it should be said that my work was done on the principle of recording facts, and not of establishing or of refuting any theory. If the facts seen do not agree with the interpretations of other observers it is fair to lay the blame on the facts, and to avert it from myself. The reading of the facts here adopted is, of course, open to any criticism and amendment. It was adopted as the simplest, and the most practicable, from a mapping point of view.

The earliest section of Dunwich cliff seems to be by R. C. TAYLOR, in a plate given in his paper " On the Geology of East Norfolk,"[*] which shows this cliff as consisting mostly of Drift, underlain by a thin bed of Crag, in its turn resting on London Clay or Plastic Clay [=Reading Beds]. There is, however, no description in the text, and so one cannot tell the reason for showing a clay-base, a thing nowhere to be seen now.

It would be unfair to judge PROF. PRESTWICH by the small sketch-section in his paper,[†] made before the existence of shelly Crag in this cliff had been made public, and before our knowledge of the extent to which such Crag was altered, by the infiltration of water, and by consequent decalcification, had reached its present point. Nevertheless, the section having been published cannot be passed over. Its author notes the occurrence of Boulder Clay along the top ; but classes the underlying beds as Glacial sand and gravels (the equivalent of WOOD's Middle Glacial), except for a strip at the very base, which is classed as Westleton Beds. My reading differs essentially in throwing these last two divisions a step lower, making the Glacial gravels Westleton Beds, and the underlying sands Crag (for the greater part, at least). Probably PROF. PRESTWICH's section was drawn long before it was published, as he was unlikely to have visited the cliff after establishing his Westleton Beds and not to have seen their good development along the upper part of this cliff.

---

[*] *Phil. Mag.* ser. ii., vol. i., pp. 277, &c., &c.   (1827.)
[†] *Quart. Journ. Geol. Soc.*, vol. xxvii. pl. xx.   (1871.)

The only other author who, to my knowledge, has published an account of this cliff-section is the late MR. S. V. WOOD, Junr., but he has often noticed it, and it may be instructive to take his remarks in chronological order, so as to show how the interpretations of one observer have varied with increased knowledge.

The first of these descriptions is dated 1865,* and it gives a mere general section, showing Post-Glacial gravel overlying Middle Drift (Middle Glacial).

In the following year we have a more detailed rendering, in a section appended to a paper by his father,† to this effect :—

"Post-Glacial yellow loam, as well as a black warp, over all."
"Deep bed of post-glacial gravel, under the ruins."
i. Upper Boulder Clay, "for a few yards only, and immediately north of the ruins."
h. Middle Glacial, "very thick here (about 50 feet)."
g³. Contorted Drift, "Dark orange sand which comes up in the southern part of the cliff-section."

In a note, written on the margin of a copy of this paper, however, the author tells me that "the red sand of Dunwich Cliff base is only part of "h."

In 1872 MR. WOOD gave us a more detailed drawing of this section,‡ from which, supplemented by notes, the following account has been made :—

Post-glacial loam, in some places containing fragments of Boulder Clay, 3 to 7 feet, not shown in the drawing, in which it is included with the next.
10. Plateau Gravel. 3 cappings.
9. Upper Glacial (Boulder Clay), at one spot only, as before.
8‴ } Middle Glacial (the sands).
8″ }
6 P. Pebbly beds (the lowest division of the Lower Glacial), along the base, except where the Crag rises up.
4. Fluviomarine Crag, at the base at one part. "An irregular line of denudation parts these micaceous sands [next above the shelly bed] from the red (or orange) sand marked 6 P." [The line is probably owing only to colour-change, not to denudation.]

In 1880, MR. WOOD made some corrections to the above,§ saying that "the bed 10, where capping the lowest part of the cliff ['S] is the Contorted Drift [Lower Glacial], consisting of brickearth with patches of Chalky Clay in it [my weathered Boulder Clay], but where capping the highest, consists of this and of a bed of shingly gravel beneath it. The very small patch of 9 over which both these passed (and which I now regard as a remnant of the Till [Lower Glacial], for it graduated into 8, while the brickearth 10 is unconformable to 8) seems to have disappeared by the waste of the coast; and 8″ and 8‴ . . . . are the sand b¹ [of this paper = Bure Valley Beds], No. 6 being either this sand as represented there or the Crag." Again he speaks of these Bure Valley, or pebbly, sands as forming "the whole or, at any rate, the upper part of the sands of Dunwich Cliff."

It will be seen that this is a radical change from the views of 1872, and approximates to my own view, formed in 1878–80, as regards the lower beds, and which was communicated to him.

In 1882,‖ our author says, that "the capping loam of Dunwich Cliff" is "a morainic bed formed . . . from a reconstruction of the pebbly sand, No. 6, with some admixture of the chalky clay [Boulder Clay] . . . . by the ice in its passage to the sea after this part of Suffolk had emerged towards the close of the chalky clay formation." He also repeats the

* In a section drawn with "A Map of the Upper Tertiaries in the Counties of Norfolk, Suffolk . . . ." Privately printed.
† Quart. Journ. Geol. Soc., vol. xxii. pp. 548. 550.
‡ With the Map in the "Supplement to the Crag Mollusca . . . . Part 1." Section R. and pp. xi., xxix., xxx. Palæontograph. Soc.
§ Quart. Journ. Geol. Soc., vol. xxxvi. p. 466, footnote, and p. 467.
‖ "Third Supplement to the Crag Mollusca . . ." p. 29. Palæontograph. Soc.

correction in the above, in the omission of the Middle Glacial, by classing the mass of the sands with the Pebbly Series, "to which the shingle under the ruins . . . also belongs; and this shingle is still more largely present in that sand at the southern end of the cliff:" thus making another step in my direction. "The whole of Dunwich Cliff," he continues, "from below the beach line up to the capping loam, is thus formed of No. 6, the intercalation of clay shown . . . by the figure 9 [Boulder Clay] being probably a modification of the sandy formation, by the introduction of argillaceous material analogous to that which gave rise to the Cromer Till and Contorted Drift of North Norfolk; both of which are, in my view, merely modifications of the same shingly sand by the introduction of a different sediment."

This view is also enforced in a paper of the same year, in different words, though to the same effect.[*]

At various times MR. WOOD was kind enough to give me drawings of this cliff-section, or of part of it. These support his later views, though noting the cliff as seen in 1866, and the only addition made to the account is in the division of the sands, which make up the greater part of the cliff, thus :—

> White or light-yellow finely stratified sand, divided by a red or orange-coloured band, beginning at the base of the pebbly gravel S. of the church, and sloping down northward to the foot of the cliff, at the end.
>
> Orange-coloured or red sand (in the central or southern parts, but hidden near the church), which may be either Bure Valley Beds or decalcified Crag.

In a letter, dated 17th January 1881, MR. WOOD also told me that he had lately had the good fortune to see shelly Crag, rising in a small boss through the beach not more than three furlongs from the southern end of the cliff, and that, besides shells, he got an equine tooth from it. As far as I know this observation has not been published.

Considering the changes that took place in his views, one may venture to hope that, had Mr. Wood's life been spared for some years, he might have come to hold my opinions; for some of his own seem to me to be somewhat forced. No one who puts a fair value on the power of actions that occur from the surface to a moderate extent downward, by the infiltration of water, etc., can doubt either that the stony loam of the cliff-top is simply weathered decalcified Boulder Clay, or that the unfossiliferous sands may be simply decalcified Crag. Examples of both these products are common enough. Moreover, a change of colour in the midst of a mass of sand is unsafe as an indication of change of bed.

Of the small lenticular patch of Boulder Clay which MR. WOOD recorded as going beneath the pebbly gravel, for a little way (north of the church) one can say nothing, never having seen it; but it seems to me possible to explain such an occurrence without assuming that the Boulder Clay is the older of the two, for that formation is one that has intrusive habits, and sometimes gets itself jammed into other beds, so as to give a delusive appearance of underlying them. All the Boulder Clay seen by me, and this was vastly more than that recorded by MR. WOOD, was most

---

[*] *Quart. Journ. Geol. Soc.*, vol. xxxviii., pp. 737, 738.

clearly above the pebbly gravel, and not for a little way only, but for a good distance, as my colleagues, MR. H. B. WOODWARD and MR. J. H. BLAKE, can testify.

In his letter of January 1881, MR. WOOD refers to the loss of the clay, beneath the gravel, by the cutting-back of the cliff since 1866; but he also mentions that a fresh clearance showed a bed of clay, up to six feet thick " stratified or laminated in part, and unstratified and unlaminated in other parts " in such a position; and the drawing he gives, makes this clay wedge off northward in the top part of the sand. This description, however, is not that of a Boulder Clay, but agrees rather with that of the clayey beds just recorded as occurring at one place, at the base of the Pebbly Series.

With the conclusion adopted by MR. H. B. WOODWARD,* in which I believe he is joined by MR. J. H. BLAKE, that the pebbly gravel here, and at Westleton, is simply part of Mr. Wood's Middle Glacial, my reading by no means agrees. This gravel or its continuation, seems to underlie deposits that belong to Mr. Wood's Lower Glacial, as already noted, and as will be noted hereafter (see p. 63, etc.), whilst, on the other hand, it has not been found overlying such. Again, it seems that in this cliff, and else-where in the district, there is a feeble representation of Mr. Wood's Middle Glacial, above the Pebbly Series.

## General Section.

In closing the account of this interesting cliff it may be well perhaps to throw the results arrived at into the form of a generalised section, with the classification of the beds that seems most practicable. With this description, and the section, in hand, future observers can then both easily record fresh points, not seen by me, and correct any mistakes that have been made.

1. Soil and wash—

Glacial Drift.
2. Boulder Clay, decomposing to a stony loam, which latter alone generally occurs where there is little of the bed.
3. Sand; local and thin, in the central part only: probably = Middle Glacial of Wood.
4. Laminated clay; very local and thin, at one place in the central part only: possibly Glacial brickearth [? part of Lower Glacial of Wood].

Pebbly Series.
5. Pebbly gravel and sand, sometimes thick.
6. Laminated clay and sand, with some pebbles, partly broken up; very local and thin, at one place in the northern part only.

Upper Crag.
7. Sands, light-coloured and ferruginous : the top few feet sometimes stony, and of doubtful classification (massed with Crag on account of the impossibility of mapping separately); the rest probably decalcified Crag, and ranging throughout the cliffs (except where talus hides the lower part of the section nearer the southern end); thick.
8. Shelly sand : very rarely seen at the foot of the cliff, or under the beach.

---

* *Geol. Mag.*, dec. ii., vol. ix., p. 455, 456 (1882).

It may be noted that the three thin local beds (3, 4, 6) seem to have escaped notice before.  Though small matters, the upper two seem to me to have some importance in the question of classification. Can the lowest represent the clay which Mr. Wood saw, in another part, below the gravel ?—

## SOUTHWOLD, 1878–1880, WITH NOTES OF EARLIER ACCOUNTS.

The southern part of this cliff, Gun Hill, is overgrown, but consists of pebbly gravel and sand.

A little beyond the next opening, South Green, light-coloured sand was just seen, as also by the Sailors' Reading Room, at the end of East Street, where there seems to be gravel at the base.

Sand, and a little gravel, were also shown at the next opening (East Green, East Cliff Villa).

At St. James' Terrace, the next opening, there was nothing clear ; but by the Coast Guard Station, at its northern side, sand and gravel were just shown.  This was the end of the town on the north.

The cliff was then turfed ; but just before getting to 100 yards from the Coast Guard flagstaff, there was seen at top a little sandy pebble-gravel over light-coloured sand, some feet deep.

At 200 yards from the flagstaff a pit, dug into the cliff, gave the following section at its southern part :—

Sandy gravelly soil, and sand with layers of pebbly gravel, about 6 feet.
Light-coloured sharp sand, 8 feet seen ; but the bottom part of the pit hidden.

Like beds occurred in the central part of the small pit ; but at the north-eastern part, under the soil, there was sand, and loam with scattered stones, and in parts some clay (? weathered Boulder Clay), but the relation of these to the other beds was not clear.

Up to this, apparently there is nothing else in these low cliffs, but the pebbly gravel and sand ; but now there is more variety. Almost touching the pit just noticed, and only 30 yards further from the flagstaff, was another cut, overgrown at first, though showing Boulder Clay, but, after another 10 yards, clear from top to bottom for some 15 yards further (measured along the beach), the section being curved, and with a length of about 25 yards. The section here, which I saw very often in passing, and was, therefore, able to note thoroughly, is shown in Fig. 6 ; and it is of interest, not only from the occurrence of the shelly bed at the bottom, so like the ordinary Crag (with which one may venture to class it), but also from the change of character of the lower mass of Boulder Clay in so short a distance ; a change which should make one cautious as to making divisions in the Drift from mere lithological differences.

MR. S. V. WOOD, Junr., classed the shelly bed with his Bure Valley Beds, rather than with the Crag.  It seems not to have been laid open until just before my arrival at Southwold, in 1878.

MR. H. H. FRENCH tells me that in 1887 this section was hidden, the pit having been disused for two or three years.

FIG. 6.

*Section in the Cliff, about 250 yards N.N.E. of the Coast Guard
Flagstaff, at the Northern End of Southwold.* 1878, 1879.

S.W.                                                            N.E.

*f.*

*a.* Sandy stony soil, about a foot.

Glacial
Drift.

*b′.* Boulder Clay, weathered at top and with pipey masses of
sand, rather dark, over 3 feet, passing on the right into :—

*b.* Pale grey Boulder Clay, up to 4 feet (or more?).

*c.* Light-coloured and brown sand, mostly coarse, sometimes a
coarse grit, with gravelly layers; over 3 feet; passing into
the next. ? = the Middle Glacial sand of Wood.

*d.* Sandy pale Boulder Clay (in the central part of the pit): on
the left rather a loam and sand, with scattered stones; about
8 feet. Apparently the equivalent of the Cromer Till,
Norwich Brickearth, or Stony loam of the North Suffolk
Coast, and of Norfolk.

*e.* Gravel, chiefly of pebbles of flint, but many of chalk; some
broken shells; nearly a foot. Differs from the pebbly gravel
of the district in containing chalk.

*f.* Crag? Coarse ferruginous sand with broken shells, and so full of flint-
pebbles as to be almost a gravel. Dug to a depth of 6 feet. Of course
it is possible that this may be a shelly condition of the pebbly gravel;
but the undoubted Crag hereabouts often contains gravel. For the list
of fossils *see* pp. 82–84.

Beyond this the cliff was again overgrown, and it gets lower. Over
80 yards on, the footpath, across the fields, from the church, comes to the
shore, and a little further there begins an old pit, for the neighbouring
brickyard. At 150 yards (beyond the section figured above) part of this pit is
deeper, and at top there is brown clay and loam with stones (probably weathered
Boulder Clay). At the further end a small piece was clear and showed washy
gravel over (and sharply piped into) grey brick-clay, some of which (at the
bottom) is cream-coloured and calcareous. This clay is without stones and is
the bed which has been observed as lying above the Boulder Clay, and in which
bones have been found, at the brickyard (see p. 43). The top of the pit at this
end is at about the same level as the top of the beach close by. The section
must have been clearer in 1887, when MR. FRENCH noted the following
succession, at one part:—

Gravelly soil; 2 feet.

Hard reddish sandy clay, full of stones, and with lumps of mottled clay;
3 to 4 feet; resting irregularly on the next.

Grey clay, full of pieces of chalk and with some flints [Boulder Clay];
seen to 4 feet.

---

The geological literature of this short line of cliff is short also. The earliest
notice that I have seen is by Dr. J. MITCHELL, in the following words:—" In
the sea cliff a quarter of a mile north of Southwold, in Suffolk, the clay
[Boulder Clay] contains a bed of sand two feet thick,"* which probably
refers to the sand between the two Boulder Clays in my section.

* *Proc. Geol. Soc.*, vol. iii., no. 59, p. 4 (1838).

In a letter, written in 1878, Mr. S. V. Wood, Jun., told me that the Post-Glacial brickearth at the northern end of Southwold cliff was distinctly shown resting on Boulder Clay in 1866, and in a section (and explanation) appended to his father's paper, published in that year,* he observes that "the cliff is too obscure to show whether the sand forming much of it is *h* [=Middle Glacial], or is post-glacial; but at the north end (at the kiln) *i* [=Boulder Clay] together with thick post-glacial beds capping it, and containing freshwater shells, has been thrown nearly into the vertical."

In 1871, Prof. Prestwich gave a figure of the northern end of this cliff, showing the following succession, the upper two beds being drawn as cutting across the lowest bed, from top to bottom.†

|  | Feet. |
|---|---|
| "Brick-earth and gravel, with the remains of *Elephas primigenius*. | 5 to 10 |
| Boulder Clay (upper division) | 8 to 12 |
| White and yellow sand and shingle, with a few ferruginous bands | 20" |

In his general section (pl. xx.) the cliff is shown as consisting of his Westleton Beds, underlain by Chillesford Clay for the most part, and cut off by later beds (as above) at the north. I believe, however, that Chillesford Clay has never been seen here, and probably it has been cut off by the pebbly gravel, as at the southern part of Easton Cliff.

---

* *Quart. Journ. Geol. Soc.*, vol. xxii., pp. 548, 550.
† *Quart. Journ. Geol. Soc.*, vol. xxvii., p. 462.

## CHAPTER 8. CLIFF SECTIONS (*continued*).

### EASTON BAVENT.

#### (*LINE 3 OF THE PLATE.*)

*Description of the Section as seen in* 1878 *and after.*

This line of cliffs, which begins on the northern side of the Buss Creek, Southwold, and ends at the southern side of Easton Broad, is barely separated into three, by the little valley running northwestward, from north of the farm, to the marshes, and by what little remains of another valley at the Broad.

The following description may vary somewhat (though only in trifles) from the plate, for the cutting-back of the cliff, since the drawing was made, has resulted in taking the lower beds to a somewhat higher level, presumably from a slight rise inland.

---

The notable points in the southern division of the cliff are the evenness of the junction of the Pebbly Series and the Chillesford Beds, in distinction to its irregular character in many other places, and the erosive junction of the patches of Drift with the Pebbly Series, an occurrence the more important if, as I believe, we have in those patches part of the lower division of the Glacial Drift, and not merely the Upper Boulder Clay alone.

At the southern end, where the ground got clear of the shingle, there was, for a short way, a little sandy and gravelly black soil, with sand coming up beneath. This was, for some way, below the level of the highest fall of beach.

As the ground rises, sand with layers of pebbly gravel is shown, until, some 40 yards on, this is cut into by a hollow of irregular loam sand and clay, with various stones, and some small bits of shell (?), a deposit like the stony loam or sandy Boulder Clay of the Southwold section, and which ended in about 25 yards. The high tides had cleared away much of the shingle in front of this hollow, in November 1879, and left a small low cone of stony-loam and Boulder Clay sticking up through the shingle a few yards in front of the cliff.

Hence for about 200 yards, the base being more or less hidden by talus, nothing but the Pebbly Series was seen, and it consisted of sand, with layers of pebbly gravel, forming a sandy gravel, at top, at the higher part. The sand is often false-bedded, in great part brown, but light-coloured also.

Then, the base being clear of talus for a little way, there was seen, beneath the pebbly sand, firm and sometimes hard ferruginous false-bedded sand, to a height of 5 feet. This is much like decalcified Crag; but in the absence of any evidence it is better to take it as part of the series above. This clean piece ran for about 75 yards further, and the section of the upper beds is as follows :—

Gravel with sand, passing down into
Sand with gravel,      ,,      ,,      ,,
False-bedded light-coloured sand, with few stones.

About 60 yards further, at my first visit (in 1878), the base was again clear, and I saw the ferruginous sand abutting against laminated clay and loam, which clearly belonged to the Chillesford Beds; but whether the bottom sand goes under or over the clay it was impossible to tell ; so that its classification (as part of the Pebbly Series, or as Crag) is doubtful. Since then this part of the base of the cliff has been hidden. The Chillesford Beds here were seen to a height of about 3 feet, and consisted chiefly of brown laminated clay, with layers of sand at the base.

Speaking probably of a part of the section near here, MR. G. MAW has noticed that "in the cliff between Southwold and Easton-Bavent . . . . a surface layer of peaty gravel has bleached the bright yellow sands overlying the Chillesford clay to a depth of ten or twelve feet—the light-grey sands under the carbonaceous surface-layer joining on to the golden-yellow sands in the bottom of the section with an outline not corresponding with stratification." This bleaching is thought to have been brought about by the action of percolating water, with organic matter in solution, which has carried down the oxide of iron of the colouring-matter.*

From about 50 yards beyond the abrupt junction of sand and clayey beds, the base of the cliff was for the most part clear at one time or other, so that one was enabled to trace the beds, with comparatively slight gaps, the base of the pebbly beds being seen throughout, except just at first. At my earlier visits however the Crag sand was not seen along the foot more than a few yards south of the ruins of the farm ; but in September 1880 the beach was lower, and the sand was shown southward, nearly to the Drift-hollow described below. Perhaps too the beds may rise slightly inland, in which case the cutting-back of the cliff would show lower beds.

At first the section was thus :—

> Pebbly Series. Light-coloured sand, with irregular beds of gravel about the middle, ferruginous at the bottom part, and at the base often with a gravel-layer.
>
> Chillesford Beds { Clay, 3½ feet.
> { Sand and clay, ½ foot.

Just north, masses of gravel come on in the midst of the sand, and then these, with the overlying sand, were cut through by a hollow of Drift. This hollow, when seen best (in 1878, 1879) was about 110 yards northward of the first ridge (=remains of hedge) south of the farm, or 190 yards southward from the southern hedge of the farm. It consisted of a central mass of clay, like weathered Boulder Clay, enwrapped with brown sand ; the outer part being irregular loam and sand, with stones, like the stony loam of Southwold cliff. The Drift-hollow at that time cut through the gravel a little way into the sand beneath ; but in May 1882 it was smaller, from the cutting-back of the cliff, not going half way down from the surface to the top of the Chillesford Clay, and no divisions were shown. In August 1887 it was 10 feet deep and 44 feet broad, according to MR. FRENCH, who then found a thin mass of Drift beginning over 60 yards to the north, and reaching nearly to the ruined farm.

25 or 30 yards beyond the hollow of Drift the section taken at various times was as follows, the lower beds being noted in 1880 (when they came to a higher level) and this section continued further north.

> Sand and gravel, with 1 to 1½ feet of fine sandy gravel at the base.
>
> Chillesford Beds { Clay, more sandy at the base, 5 feet or more.
> { Sand with clay-layers in the lower part, 5 feet or more.

About 50 yards beyond the Drift-hollow the Pebbly Series consisted of sand with layers and lines of gravel, whilst a little further it was a mass of gravel, with sand above and below. Still further, under the ruins of the farm, there was little sand above, and that below was gravelly at the base. It should be remembered that this farm has now gone (except remains of foundation).

The Chillesford Beds here showed, at places, the following succession : Brown clay and loam ; dark grey clay and loam ; brown loam passing down into sand : sometimes there were sandy layers in the top part.

Hence the beds rise slightly northward, so that those at the base of the cliff are better seen.

Beyond the farm the Chillesford Clay had in places an ochreous stain. At 60 or 70 yards from the farm the Pebbly Series consisted of gravel passing

---

* *Quart. Journ. Geol. Soc.*, vol. xxiv., pp. 375-378.

down into sand, and at about 100 yards the top foot or 1½ feet of the Chillesford Beds was more sand than clay.

About 140 yards north of the farm, in June 1879, the sand at the base of the cliff was seen to a depth of 5 feet, with a layer of shells 2 feet down, and the bottom 2 feet being full of shells: there were also some small pebbles and some phosphatic nodules.

Some 20 yards further the Chillesford Beds were made up as follows, each layer passing down into that below :—

    *a.* Sand, bedded with thin layers of clay, about a foot.
    *b.* Grey and brown laminated clay, about a foot.
    *c.* Bluish-grey clay, about 2½ feet.
    *d.* Brown clay with sand, ? a foot.
    Apparently sand below.

About 50 yards further on some of these divisions varied in thickness, *a* being 4 feet, *b* over a foot, *c* as before, and *d* 2 feet.

As the ground slopes down northward the Pebbly Beds end off, that process being brought about sooner by the coming on of a thin wash of loam and gravel, which at last cuts through them and rests on the Chillesford Beds. Here there was a waved junction between the divisions *b* and *c* of the latter, a point of some moment, as a like junction, further north, may partly have led Mr. S. V. Wood, Junr., to divide these beds and to regard their upper part as belonging to his Lower Glacial.

The cliff now gets very low, and, from the slight rise of the beds, the Chillesford Clay soon ends, and we have only Crag sand, which is here shell-less, probably because more open to the action of surface waters. At and near where the clay ends off the section of the Crag was as follows :—

    Loose buff or brown sand, with 2 or 3 lines of stones; over 3 feet.
    Firmer sand, bedded with loamy layers or with thin clay-layers; about 2½ feet seen.

The gravelly character of the Crag here is noteworthy, especially as sub-angular flints form a large proportion of the stones, giving the whole a newer Drift-like look. Further on the upper part is still more gravelly, so that at first I thought there might be a wash of gravel and sand in the little valley, of which however there is only a little at the top. Sometimes the upper part of the sand is bedded, and the lower part shows fine false-bedding.

In December 1879 the beach was much swept away from in front of the little hollow, so that a little soil and gravel were seen over Crag sand.

---

Beyond this gap, of about 50 yards, the ground rises quickly, the beds are at first flat, and then dip slightly northward, so that, before reaching the far end, the shelly Crag sand is lost beneath the beach, never again to appear, unless represented by the Wey-bourn Crag, of the Cromer cliff-section, a disputed point, which there is no reason to discuss here. The small patches of gravel and sand at part of the base of Pakefield cliff have yielded no shells; but their stratigraphical position, beneath the Chillesford Beds, is clear.

A noteworthy point in this second part of the Easton section is the thickening of the Chillesford Beds, presuming that all the clayey beds are rightly classed therewith.

Another is the uneven junction of the Pebbly Gravel and the Chillesford Beds, as compared with the even one of the southern section. Moreover it is where the lower series is thick that we should least expect this irregularity, rather than where it is thin, and therefore, presumably, more eroded.

When the cutting-back of the coast at the gap has reached less than another 100 yards the piece of land of which this cliff gives a perfect section will be, like Southwold, an island, connected with the mainland only by a shingle-beach.

At the beginning of this part of the cliff the Crag consists of bedded sand with gravelly layers (some large flints were seen) and sometimes with shells in the upper part.

Some 65 yards from the start shelly Crag was again seen at the base, and from about 30 yards further on layers of shells and scattered shells were seen in the gravelly sand for a distance of about 75 yards. By the further end of this exposure the section is thus :—

Pebbly Series, ⎰ Gravel at top.
7 feet, or more. ⎱ Bedded sand, with two gravel-layers at the bottom part.
Chillesford ⎰ Bedded sand and clay, 7 feet.
Beds. ⎱ Bedded clay, 5 feet.
Crag. Sand, with three layers of shells, the top one a foot thick and with pebbles, 3 feet and more seen.

A little further the Pebbly Series consists chiefly of sand, with gravel-lines in the bottom part, and still further, of gravel over false-bedded sand.

About 270 yards from the beginning, sand with shells was again seen at the foot, and beyond this the junction of the sand and gravel at top with the underlying sand and loam was seen to be irregular and apparently disturbed.

From more than 50 to nearly 80 yards further, at the highest part of the cliff there is only a thin irregular capping of gravel, the underlying loamy beds rising almost to the top.

A section measured by MR. E. T. DOWSON in November 1867, with a copy of which he has favoured me, must be from about this spot, although described as a third of a mile along the coast north of the farmhouse on the cliff; for that distance lands us near the bottom of the little valley, where the cliff is low. The beds noted were as follows :—

|  |  | Ft. | In. |
|---|---|---|---|
| Warp [soil] . . . . . | . | 1 | 0 |
| [Pebbly Series.] Sand with veins of gravel . | . | 3 | 0 |
| [Chillesford Beds.] Laminated clay, sandy above . | . | 18 | 0 |
| [Crag, about 7¾ feet]. ⎰ Sand without shells . . | . | 1 | 6 |
| Shell bed . . . | . | 0 | 9 |
| Sand with but few shells . | . | 2 | 3 |
| Shell-bed . . . | . | 0 | 4 |
| ⎱ Sand . . . | . | 3 | 0 |

From this it seems that at this earlier date the Crag reached a little higher up than now.

The pebbly gravel soon gets thicker again, cutting into the sand and loam beneath, which pass down into laminated clay; but, about 130 yards before reaching the bottom of the hollow that ends this division of the cliff, the gravel again ends off, and for some yards there is nothing but pockets, or a wash, of it over the loam of the Chillesford Beds, which here form the whole of the cliff. Just above the base of the cliff were some shells in the clay, the only such occurrence that I was fortunate enough to see, though PROF. PRESTWICH found a number of shells in the Chillesford Clay of this cliff (see p. 68).

About 100 yards from the end of the cliff gravel again comes on at top, for some 25 yards, and the following section was taken here :—

Soil and gravel (washy) about 4-feet.
Chillesford ⎰ Light-brown loam and clayey sand, passing down into the next, nearly 3 feet.
Beds. ⎱ Darker (damper) sand, with layers of clay, passing down into the next, about 3 feet.
Bedded and laminated clay, 7 feet.

In the bottom of the little hollow a miniature cliff of clay, only a few inches high, was seen, with sand and shingle washed over.

The most northerly division of this cliff, separated from the last only for about a distance of 20 yards, consists wholly of the

Chillesford Beds, and it is notable for the waved bedding in the lower and more clayey part, whilst the more sandy upper part has the bedding-planes horizontal. This piece of cliff reached only for about 160 yards in 1878, and, as the coast is cut back, it will decrease in length and in heighth, and at length will disappear. But two years or so before my visit it was joined to the main cliff (see p. 70).

## Notes of other Descriptions.

In 1866 The REV. O. FISHER alluded to this cliff, and described its lower part as " Chillesford Clay underlain by the Mya-bed," a name which he gives to a bed of sand, some seven feet below the Chillesford Clay, by Chillesford church, in which the shells of *Mya* occur in their burrows ; but he found no such occurrence here, only single valves of the shell.

He goes on to say that "immediately beneath the Chillesford Clay we came upon a band of drifted shells, two or three inches thick, containing flints and fragments of bone imbedded in a coarse sand, and, beneath this, sand with *Tellinæ* as they lived. The bed occurs . . . . at the very bottom of the second cliff north of the farm-house, and was only visible for a few feet, the rest being observed by talus."[*]

The view put forward in this paper, to the effect that the downward succession in this neighbourhood is Norwich Crag, Chillesford Clay, and Mya-bed, has been recanted by the author ; and it is to be hoped that the additional name of Mya-bed given to our already over-christened Crag may be allowed to lapse.

With the general interpretation of this cliff given by PROF. PRESTWICH in 1871,[†] the foregoing details agree ; but the use of the term Chillesford Sand for the Crag here, is objectionable ; as it is not clear how this particular bed is to be divided from the rest of the Crag. PROF. PRESTWICH'S figure seems to refer only to the southern part of the section, in which the beds rise slightly northward, as in the northern part their inclination is reversed. The Chillesford Clay however does not reach to the southern end ; but here, as in the case of Dunwich, the figure is only a generalization.

Our author was however fortunate in seeing three things here which are not generally to be seen, in one case indeed having recorded an occurrence that has not been noticed elsewhere, and his remarks will therefore be quoted :—

"In the . . . . cliff, at Easton Bavent, we find the same sand and shingle [as at Southwold], with seams of the ferruginous bed. In the latter, casts of shells are numerous, but difficult of determination. I found *Cardium, Mytilus (edulis ?), Littorina, Natica*, and numbers of small Foraminifera." . . . . . .

"This section clearly shows not only the relation of these divisions [Pebbly Series, Chillesford Clay, and Crag], but in the same cliff, a short distance further north . . . . may be seen the setting-in of the Forest-bed and its relation to the same [Pebbly] series."[‡]

---

[*] *Quart. Journ. Geol. Soc.*, vol. xxii., p. 26.
[†] *Quart. Journ. Geol. Soc.*, vol. xxvii., pl. xx.
[‡] *Quart. Journ. Geol. Soc.*, vol. xxvii., p. 462.

The following section, near the northern end of the cliff, is then given :—

[Pebbly Series.] White and yellow sand and shingle, 5 feet.
[Sign of Forest Bed.] Traces of wood and carbonaceous matter.
Chillesford Clay, laminated, grey, with double shells in the position of life,
    6 feet.
[Crag.] Shelly sands.

I was unable, from the change in the cliff caused by loss of land, to find any trace of casts of shells in the ferruginous layers of the Pebbly Series, or any sign of the carbonaceous line referred to the Forest Bed. Of shells in the Chillesford Clay only a few were noticed, at one spot and on one day only.

In the second of his Crag papers PROF. PRESTWICH also refer to this section and says "along part of the cliff I found no organic remains in the clay ; but at the more northern end of the cliff I met with them at one spot in considerable abundance—many with double valves . . . . . *Leda myalis* was common."* (*see* List, pp. 82–84.)

The only other author to be referred to is MR. S. V. WOOD, Junr, who has often noticed this cliff, and first, in 1866, described the general section as showing the following succession :—†

Post-Glacial loam, at the northern end (p. 551).
*h.* Middle Glacial (sand and gravel).
*g³.* Contorted Drift (Lower Glacial, loam).
*f.* Bure Valley Beds (sand and shingle).
*e'.* Chillesford Clay.
*e.* Chillesford shell-bed (sand).

In 1872 our author gave a drawing of the whole section (with further detail at one spot)‡ in which the cliff, in two parts, is shown as consisting of the beds noted in the table below.

| Beds. | Southern Cliff. | Northern Cliff. |
|---|---|---|
| 10. Plateau Gravel - - | Patch, on N., by valley - | Two patches, at southern and central parts. |
| 8. Middle Glacial - - | Patch, just N. of the following. | — |
| 7. Contorted Drift - - | Patch, at middle part - | At top, along N. half. |
| 6. Pebbly Beds - - | Throughout, except at N. end. | In southern part. |
| 5. Chillesford Beds ; divided into clay above and sand [ = Crag] below in the detailed section, in which too instead of 10 we have 11, = Post-Glacial Valley Gravel (? a slip). | Along the base, except at the south. | All along the lower part. |

In 1877 MR. WOOD speaks of the Contorted Drift of the northern cliff as doubtful.§

In 1880, referring to the Covehithe cliff and to the two cliffs of Easton, he remarks that "these are all formed by the Chillesford Clay in its greatest thickness, overlain by the red and orange-coloured beds belonging to the lower part of the pebbly sand—the uppermost sands of the Crag, which are white and full of shells, coming up under the clay only in the central one of these three cliffs," by which it is clear that he was never fortunate enough to

---

* *Quart. Journ. Geol. Soc.*, vol. xxvii., p. 345.
† *Quart. Journ. Geol. Soc.*, vol. xxii., pp. 547, 548, 551.
‡ Sections S. and VII., with the Map, in the Supplement to the Crag Mollusca, Part I. *Palæontograph. Soc.*
§ *Quart. Journ. Geol. Soc.*, vol. xxxiii., p. 102.

see the base of the northern part of the southern cliff clear, showing these sands. He continues : "at the south end of the southernmost cliff of Eastern [Easton] Bavent the Chillesford Clay has been cut away, and its place taken by the pebbly sands,"* as shown in the section and alluded to in the above description (p. 63).

In 1882 MR. WOOD changed his views as to some of the beds, giving a very different interpretation to part of the section. He says, "I found that the bed which in the representation of Easton-Bavent 'cliff' in the Introduction to the first Supplement to my father's 'Monograph of the Crag Mollusca' was shown as the Contorted Drift . . . . . . is really the moraine of a stream of ice which issued from the great inland ice-field at the close of the Chalky-Clay [Upper Boulder Clay] formation in East Suffolk, this moraine being a reconstruction of the Chillesford Clay on which it rests, and of some of the pebbly sand . . . . which had covered that clay, and over which this ice-stream had passed"; to which is added the footnote "This is adjoining Easton Broad; and a close inspection of it is necessary to see its distinctness from the Chillesford Clay."† The two small hollows of Drift in the southern cliff also follow the same classification, as well apparently as the clay, &c. in Southwold cliff (Fig. 6, p. 61), and these conclusions are repeated in the same year in other words.‡ The bed classed as Contorted Drift (Lower Glacial) of the earlier sections, is, therefore, now classed as Upper Glacial.

It is not, however, from his published works only that MR. WOOD's views are known, for, as with Dunwich, so with Easton he kindly gave me drawings of his sections on a large scale, showing details, some of which, having been noted at an earlier time, differ from mine, and may therefore be noticed.

Along the southern cliff a fairly continuous but thin capping of gravel and sand is shown, and classed as either Post Glacial or Middle Glacial (decidedly as the latter in one drawing); but one is inclined to think that this is merely the somewhat altered surface part of the Pebbly Series, the only clear deposit of the sort that I could see being the small gravelly wash near the northern end.

On either side of the hollow of Drift, by the highest part of the cliff, gaps are shown, that on the north reaching almost to the base of the cliff.

These gaps had disappeared at the time of my first visit, by the cutting-back of the cliff, as also had a third, further north, somewhere near the farm.

In my time, however, the foot of the cliff must have been much clearer than when seen by MR. WOOD, whose sections show mere patches of Chillesford Clay, a little south of the farm, the greater part being hidden by talus.

Of the Pebbly Series the following succession of beds is given :—

Shingle beds and sand, interbedded with red bedded sand.
Yellow or orange-coloured sand, with little or no shingle.
Yellow or orange-coloured bedded sand, with shingle bands.

Along the northern cliff again thin cappings of Middle Glacial or Post Glacial gravel are shown, cappings that I believe to belong to the Pebbly Series.

---

* Quart. Journ. Geol. Soc., vol. xxxvi., p. 467.
† Quart. Journ. Geol. Soc., vol. xxxviii., p. 737.
‡ Third Supplement to the Crag Mollusca, p. 22.

The loamy bed next underlying this gravel at the central part, and forming the upper half at the northern part, is described as yellowish-brown or tawny sandy loam, unstratified, and contorted in places, and it is classed as Contorted Drift, a classification given up in 1882, when the age of the bed was taken to be Upper rather than Lower Glacial (see above).

The Chillesford Clay is shown, as in my section, to form half or more of this cliff at the southern part (where the gravel above is classed with the Pebbly Series), and the following divisions in it are noted :—

Ash-coloured clay.
Sandy band.
Ash-coloured clay, in places having contortions.
Dark blue laminated clay, with shells of *Tellina* and *Mactra*, and some rolled pieces of chalk.

When engaged in the survey of the district to the north, in 1875 (and later), Mr. J. H. BLAKE visited this cliff, in order to compare the beds shown with those of Kessingland, etc., and he drew the section to a horizontal scale but little less than that used by me and to a larger vertical scale. He sent me his drawing whilst this Memoir was passing through the press, and from it I have been enabled to take out from the plate a few patches of talus, near the site of the ruins of Easton Bavent, where he saw the cliff cleared.

Both Mr. Blake's record, and his interpretation thereof, to which he was led quite independently, agree with mine.

He saw some Boulder Clay at the Drift-hollow close to the southern end of the cliff; but the abrupt ending of the Chillesford Beds was hidden, and the second Drift hollow seems to have been hardly as clear as in my time.

He noticed that, at about the site of the ruined farm, the upper part of the Chillesford Beds had " a greenish tinge, like the Rootlet-bed at Kessingland," and, in the second cliff, a little north of the highest part, he describes the uppermost part of the same series as " unstratified brown clay and sand, mottled, with ash-coloured loam, like the Rootlet-bed .  .  .  . at Pakefield."

It is interesting to find that when Mr. BLAKE made his drawing, the cutting-back of the coast had not gone far enough to detach the small northern-most piece of cliff from the larger mass to the south; but that the two were continuous, the deepest part of the hollow which now divides them showing a cliff about 5 feet high. Three small patches of the Pebbly Series were noted at the northernmost part, which have now disappeared, from the decrease in height.

### General Remarks on the Section.

Besides the notable points to which attention has been drawn in the description of the three divisions of the cliff, there are some that are not confined to any one division. These are the generally fine-bedded or laminated character of the Chillesford Clay ; the even junction of that clay with the underlying Crag sand ; the southerly thinning of the clay, a thinning which agrees with its absence further south, over a large area ; and the comparatively evenly-bedded character of the Crag, with its gravelly layers, as distinguished from the strongly false-bedded character of the Red Crag in tracts further south, where too stones are almost confined to the nodule-bed at the base.

As my classification of the beds differs materially from all the expressed views of the late Mr. S. V. WOOD, Junr., it will be well firstly to give an epitome of the beds seen, according to my view, and then to justify that view. For this purpose we may disregard the small piece of cliff at the extreme north, or may group it with the rest of the northern half of the section, in regard to which the chief differences of interpretation occur, and may put the result in a tabular form.

| Beds. | Southern cliff. | Northern cliff. |
|---|---|---|
| Post Glacial.  Wash of loam and gravel. | Of no moment, and at one place only. | ——— |
| Glacial Drift  { Boulder Clay / Sand / Stony loam } | Two small hollows only. | ——— |
| Pebbly Series.  Sand and gravel. | Throughout, except at extreme northern end. | At top mostly, at higher parts. |
| Chillesford Beds.  Loam and clay. | Throughout, except at southern end. | Throughout. |
| Crag.  Sand with gravel-layers and shells. | Along foot of greater part. Not S. | Along foot of southern half. |

Practically therefore these cliffs are taken to consist of three deposits only, the Pebbly Series, the Chillesford Beds, and the Crag, the rest being mere local dots.

Comparing this with MR. WOOD'S versions it will be seen that at all events my view has one advantage, that of simplicity; as it practically gets rid of various divisions with which Mr. Wood classifies deposits that occur for some distance, those divisions being limited (in my view) to mere patches, only one of which could be barely shown on the map, and that one probably is now lost, by the cutting-back of the cliff. The divisions in question are as follows, with the reasons for rejecting them :—

1. *Post-Glacial Gravel*, or *Plateau Gravel*. All the gravel, above the Chillesford Beds, in these cliffs seemed to me to belong to one series, being all of one character.

2. *Upper Glacial.* (*Contorted Drift* of the earlier accounts.) The small core of Boulder Clay seen in the Drift-hollow at the middle part of the southern cliff is practically nothing; indeed it seems to have disappeared. For Mr. Wood's classification (1882) of the loams next beneath the gravel of the northern part of the northern cliff as of this age, there seems no reason, other than the theoretical views brought forward by him in his latest works referring to this district, views which may have influenced his judgment in the interpretation of facts. I was unable to divide this loam from the underlying loam and clay, and felt bound to class the whole as Chillesford Beds, with PROF. PRESTWICH.

MR. J. H. BLAKE writes (May 1887) as follows :—" This loam is similar, in my opinion, to the irregular stratified part of the Rootlet-bed (Forest Bed) at Kessingland, and of the same age, passing down here into the characteristic laminated clays of the Chillesford Beds, as it does there." My colleague's view amounts practically to the same as my own, in tying on this loam to the Chillesford Beds and not to the Drift.

Any other classification makes it needful to differentiate one mass of pebbly gravel and sand from other masses of the same kind, at about the same level, and within the same limited area ; for the one mass must be regarded as overlying beds newer than the others. According to MR. WOOD'S latest interpretation the one mass of gravel must be Post Glacial, whilst the others belong to his lowest member of the Lower Glacial.

3. *Middle Glacial.* The only bed that I could class with this division of MR. WOOD is the thin layer of sand enwrapping the core of Boulder Clay in the Drift-hollow south of the farm, and which probably has now disappeared. The persistence of a thin bed of sand in this position is remarkable, and the reader is referred to the sections at Dunwich and Southwold cliffs, as well as to various others inland, where the like sand is seen.

Of course the classification of the upper loam of the northern cliff as Lower Glacial led to the overlying gravel being classed as Middle Glacial, the objection to which is the same as that just made to assigning it a Post Glacial age.

As to the *Contorted Drift*, a division abandoned by MR. WOOD in his latest classification of the beds of these cliffs, all that seems of this age (Lower Glacial) is the outer part of the northern Drift-hollow of the southern cliff, and the small southern hollow ; both of which were taken from the Lower Glacial by MR. WOOD, and classed, with the rest, as Upper Glacial. For my own part I incline to the view that these small patches belong probably to the sandy Boulder Clay, or stony loam, that in this district, seems to form the base of the Drift, leaving out of the question the possibility of the underlying Pebbly Series being classed as Drift.

To conclude, it would have been a pleasure to agree with MR. WOOD, instead of having to differ from him, in the interpretation of this and of other sections. As to the facts the only differences between us are probably due to the varying character of the section.

## COVEHITHE.

### (*LINE 4 OF THE PLATE.*)

### *Description of the Section as seen in* 1878 *and* 1879.

This, the shortest of our three coast-sections (not counting the hidden cliff of Southwold), is also the lowest, the clearest, and the simplest. It is the only one of which I have seen the base clear, from end to end ; as a rule indeed, there being no talus of great amount during the three years of my visits, in 1878–1880. It consists practically moreover of only two deposits, the Pebbly Series and the Chillesford Beds, the Drift patches being both small and evanescent, as the section alters ; but it is our longest section of the Chillesford Beds, which are but just hidden at one spot only, and then for less than 50 yards (perhaps now not at all): their base however is nowhere shown, so that the Easton Bavent section is the more perfect.

The Pebbly Series here rests in parts fairly evenly, and in others irregularly, on the Chillesford Beds.

It may be well to notice an appearance that has sometimes been seen in the Covehithe cliff, which is of a deceptive character, and might lead observers to think, at all events for a time, that they had found traces of the Forest Bed. The top part of the Chillesford Beds has, in places, been perforated by roots, the decayed remains of which often simulate the like occurrence further north, at Kessingland etc., which has been termed the "rootlet-bed," by my colleague MR. J. H. BLAKE, who has worked in so much detail over the Forest Bed. I have seen these rootlets at times, (in other parts besides the little hollow, where they occur under a recent deposit, as noticed below) once in company with MR. BLAKE, when we satisfied ourselves that here the roots were those of modern and not, as at Kessingland, of Pre Glacial plants. The deception is enhanced by the rootlets occurring beneath the pebbly gravel, that is in exactly the place where the Forest Bed would be expected. If my memory serves me rightly, in some cases the rootlets seemed to be those of plants that had grown on the face of the cliff.

In 1886 my colleague MR. C. REID also noticed this occurrence, of which he has sent me the following note, taken a little south of where the lane is cut off by the cliff:—" The upper part of the Chillesford Clay is full of small irregular tubes, filled with sand (? roots), which come just below the gravel, and reach to a depth of about 3 feet."

At first, just north of the little Broad, there was merely a few inches of sandy soil, above which shingle and sand had been driven. Then, as the ground gently rises, there was a very low cliff, about 4 feet at the highest, of loam, belonging to the Chillesford Beds, with shingle and sand, from the beach, at top, for about 60 yards.

Then gravelly patches came on above the brown loam, and then a bed of sand, more or less peaty (from the soil) with gravel at its base. This bed thickens, as the ground still rises, and, just beyond the little bank and ditch, the following succession was noted:—

Sandy soil, about 2 feet.
Pebbly Series. Yellowish false-bedded sand, with layers of gravel in the lower part.
Chillesford Beds. Bedded brown loam.

Some 40 yards beyond the bank the loam was rather contorted, and just beyond, the section was as follows:—Soil and sand, about 6 feet, over false-bedded sandy gravel, nearly 4 feet, over loam.

At and near 100 yards beyond the bank the top part of the sand was gravelly, the middle part somewhat bedded, and the lower as before.

Beyond this the top 2 feet of the loam was more sandy, and then the top of the little cliff was formed of drifted sand, and there was a curious overhanging of the upper part of this, from its having been hardened and compacted, by the soil, rootlets, &c., so that the turfed surface held together, though undercut, and spread over the edge of the cliff in a downward curve. This also occurred southward, more or less.

Just before getting to the next little ditch and bank the sand ends off, and the Chillesford loam is hidden for awhile, along the lower ground, by a hollow, filled with sand gravel and peaty alluvial loam, which reaches for 100 yards or more. This deposit is, of course, of late age, being merely a wash along the little valley.

In June 1879 the Chillesford Beds were seen, clear from beach, along the foot of the above deposit, except for about 40 yards at the southern end; and, in May 1882, when the cliff had been further cut back, at one place, in the northern part of the hollow, some rootlets were seen in the top of the loamy beds, then discoloured grey. These rootlets seemed modern; but they may serve as a caution not to be hasty in referring such an occurrence to the so-called " Forest Bed " age, unless there be further evidence, in the shape of an overlying mass of the Pebbly Series. When visiting the Kessingland coast, the very modern look of some of the " Forest Bed," with its rootlets, so like a modern river-deposit, has often struck me.

The valley-deposit runs a little up the gentle slope northward, in the form of pipes and patches of gravel, with some peaty earth; and about 30 yards beyond the hollow, beneath 2½ feet of soil and wash, came 3½ of brown (and a little grey) loam, and then 2½ of firm brown sand.

Hence, to where the gravel comes on above, the Chillesford Beds consisted of bedded brown buff and grey sand and loam; and, at the last, some carbonaceous specks and some sand of a lighter colour were seen near the bottom.

About 130 yards beyond the hollow the cliff showed soil and pebbly gravel, false-bedded in a northerly direction, to about 7 feet thick, over buff and brown bedded sand and loam, more loamy at the base; whilst just beyond, in the middle of the hollow of the Pebbly Series, the section was:—

Soil, 2 feet.
Pebbly Series { Gravelly sand, 3½ feet.
{ Gravel, 3½ feet.
Chillesford Beds.  Loam and sand, about 3½ feet.

Still further the sand alone occurs at top, except for soil, to a thickness of about 5 feet, and then the bedded sand and loam rose to the top, for a few feet, the bottom part showing a little contortion.

Just after the sand and gravel came on again there were signs of the occurrence of a loamy layer with pebbles between these and the clean loam. This thin layer was thought at first to be merely a gravelly top to the loam; but as, further on, it scoops into the beds below, I ended by classing it with the gravel.

It began first as a distinct layer, about 12 or 15 yards from the recommencement of the sand and gravel, and consisted of bedded sand and loam, with gravel at the bottom. The Pebbly Series now occurs all along the cliff, until cut off at the northern end.

At about 240 to 310 yards from the hollow the loamy condition of the Chillesford Beds seemed to end somewhat suddenly, and there was brown and yellow sand, in great part firm, looking almost as if filling a sort of hollow in the loam (which was shown beneath in places); but it seemed safer to take this as a lateral change.

At about 280 yards from the hollow the Pebbly Series consisted of gravel and sand over bright yellowish-brown sand; whilst, some 16 or 17 yards further, where the hollow of Drift loam comes on above, 6 feet of gravelly sand, over 2 feet of gravel were seen.

The hollow of loam shown here was noted in 1878, in 1879 its size was a little less, and in June 1880 it had gone altogether, by the cutting-back of the coast. I believe that the loam belonged to the lower part of the Glacial, Drift.

Hence, for some way, the Pebbly Series consisted of bedded gravel and sand sometimes with loam, and the Chillesford Beds of loam and sand, sometimes contorted, or waved, and the sand sometimes in nests in the loam.

The following section, communicated by Mr. E. T. Dowson, from a note made in July 1868, must have been measured near here, being described as a quarter of a mile south of the Coast Guard Station:—

Warp [soil], 1½ feet.
[Pebbly Series] { Sand and a few small stones, 5 feet.
{ Gravel and seams of clay, 7 feet.
[Chillesford] clay, 7 feet.

At about the spot marked C on the plate, Line 4, and some 420 yards (? more) south of the road, the section shown by Fig. C of the plate was noted in June 1880. The remarkable contortions in the upper part of the Chillesford Beds were really stronger than drawn, it being impossible (to me at least) to sketch the fine details.

Beyond this the gravel and sand was often false-bedded, for 120 yards or more. About 320 yards from the road the loamy layer, at the base of this series, set in and reached for some 60 yards, consisting of bedded loam with a gravelly layer (scattered stones) at the bottom, and cutting into the bedded sand of the underlying Chillesford Series.

This layer again occurred from about 175 to 145 yards south of the road, from about 110 to 95, and from about 25 to a little north of the road, coming on again very soon and then reaching to about 70 yards beyond the road.

Throughout this range the sand and gravel showed both bedding and false bedding, and in May 1882, a long lenticular layer of loam was noticed, in the lower part, from over 30 yards south of the road to nearly 70 north of it.

From about 55 yards south of the road to 110 north of it the Chillesford loam had its bedding much curved in the lower part.

Coming on at about 105 yards beyond the road there is shown, in the plate, a hollow of Drift loam, bedded, with gravelly sand at the base, which cuts through the Pebbly Series into the Chillesford Beds for 20 yards, and is the only break in the continuity of the last throughout the cliff. When first noting the section, in October 1878, this loam was not seen, the upper part of the cliff consisting only of the Pebbly Series : in June 1879, when the cliff had been cut back a good deal, it was shown, as drawn : but in June 1880 it had gone, from further cutting-back, and there was again only the Pebbly Series at top.

At about where this last ends off lenticular layers of sand occurred in the middle of the laminated Chillesford Clay.

At the end the beach wrapped round and rose a little way over the cliff.

### Descriptions by Mr. Wood and others.

In the section appended to his father's paper of 1866,[*] Mr. S. V. Wood, Junr., describes this cliff as consisting chiefly of Bure Valley Beds (pebbly gravel and sand) over Chillesford Clay, with the addition of a bed of Post Glacial loam at the southern end, of "a post-glacial gravel-capping . . . .", and a more recent sand in the valley-depression." Possibly too a little Contorted Drift may be included.

In the drawing of the section given in 1872[†] there seems to be a slip, the smaller part of the cliff being put on the north instead of on the south. The beds shown are as follows :—

10. Plateau Gravel, a patch at top.
7. Contorted Drift, a patch at top.
6. Pebbly Sand &c.
5. Chillesford Clay (= 5″ of Section viii.).

Mr. Wood's remarks of 1880 have been already given under Easton Bavent (p. 68). There seems some slip, however, in speaking of a mass of ¡Contorted Drift "which extended from the north of Easton to the south of Covehithe Cliff"[‡] there being a long gap between the two cliffs, through which beach only is seen.

The view of 1882, already referred to (p. 69) is extended to Covehithe, the Plateau Gravel of the section of 1872 being now taken as part of the morainic Upper Glacial bed.[§]

The drawing of this section which Mr. Wood gave me does not materially differ from the published version. It shows three thin long strips of Post Glacial, or Middle Glacial, gravel and sand, at the northern and southern slopes and filling the middle hollow, leaving indeed only the higher parts of the cliff bare. Except for this our sections differ only in the southern part being here

---

* Quart. Journ. Geol. Soc., vol. vol. xxii., pp. 547, 548, 551.
- † Supplement to the Crag Mollusca, Part I., Section S. Palæontograph. Soc.
‡ Quart. Journ. Geol. Soc., vol. xxxvi., p. 466. (footnote.)
§ Third Supplement to the Crag Mollusca, p. 22. Palæontograph. Soc.

made rather the larger, and with a longer and thicker mass of the Pebbly Series. This seems to have been through some accident (? transposition), as the configuration of the ground shows that nothing of the sort could have held within late years.

On a smaller drawing, of the southern end only, Mr. WOOD remarks that the Chillesford Clay is "contorted occasionally with small sand galls," and he notes the following divisions in it at one place :—

> Brown clay, a foot.
> Alternations of ash-coloured clay and sand, 4 feet.
> Ash-coloured clay, contorted, 4 feet.

With the small general view given by PROF. PRESTWICH[*] my observations also agree. Indeed in the case of this cliff all observers seem to have come to much the same general conclusion.

MR. BLAKE'S drawing of this cliff-section was made at the same season and on the same scales as that of Easton, above alluded to, and in this case also our views agree (except that, as also in the case of Easton, I am not sure of the presence of the Rootlet-bed, a matter which however does not affect the classification). Near the southern end he noticed a little greenish clay, in the top part of the Chillesford Series, like his Rootlet-bed; opposite the hollow he saw Crag shells washed up on the beach, though no actual Crag was seen; and, on again reaching higher ground, he again noted, beneath the pebbly gravel, something "similar in character to the Rootlet-bed at Pakefield." At this time the two hollows of Drift-loam had not been cut into.

---

The drawings of the cliff-sections made by MR. WOOD and by MR. BLAKE, which have been described in these pages, will be deposited in the Geological Survey Office. Those by Mr. Blake give a great amount of detail as to the composition of the Pebbly Series, which could only be shown with the large vertical scale adopted. These details however, are ever-varying, as the cliffs are cut back.

## KESSINGLAND.  (*Short Notice.*)

THE cliff-section here, which begins at the road south of the Coast Guard Station, has already been generally described, and figured on a large scale, by MR. J. H. BLAKE,[†] who will also give full details in the Memoir on the map to the north (67), in which the greater part of this line of cliff lies. It will be enough here therefore to notice the salient points very briefly.

At first there is Glacial Sand, to a considerable thickness, beneath which, and with an even junction, comes the Rootlet-bed (as it has been named by MR. BLAKE), which is an unstratified greenish-grey clay (the upper part sometimes brown), with race and small flints; altogether some 5 feet thick.

This is underlain by thin, buff, pebbly sand, passing down into laminated grey clay and buff sand. These belong to the Chillesford Beds, which have been seen at one place to a depth of over 12 feet, and which form the base of this part of the cliff throughout, as far as could be seen.

At the Coast Guard Station there is a patch of Boulder Clay at the top, the ground rising there; but as the ground falls again northward this soon ends.

---

[*] *Quart. Journ. Geol. Soc.*, vol. xxvii., pl. xx.
[†] Horizontal Section Sheet 128 (1884), and Explanation of that Section (1885.)

At the next rise however the clay comes on in greater force, and continues to form the upper part of the cliff for some distance, reaching a thickness of over 20 feet, whilst the sand beneath is about 30 feet thick.

The points of contrast with the foregoing sections are as follows :—

1. The absence of the Pebbly Series, or rather the local absence, as in that part of the section beyond this district MR. BLAKE has classed some thin masses of sand gravel and clay with that series.

2. The occurrence of the Rootlet-bed, showing a terrestrial surface, with rootlets reaching downwards from the top. This division has been classed with the so-called Forest Bed Series, which seems not to occur southward, though MR. BLAKE thinks that the Rootlet-bed may be partly represented in the upper part of the loam classed with the Chillesford Beds (see pp. 70, 76).

3. The presence of Glacial Sand (Middle Glacial of WOOD) in force; whereas it is absent, or but slightly represented, in the southern cliffs.

4. The on-coming of the Boulder Clay in mass. This is indeed the finest section of that deposit, showing the junction with the sand below for a long distance. The evenness of that junction is remarkable. The great variety of stones in the clay may be well seen here.

------

Postscript to *pp.* 63, 64.

MR. H. H. FRENCH tells me that, in 1887, the breadth of the small mass of Drift at the southern end of the Easton cliff had decreased to 25 feet, or to one third of that above noted; and that the storm of August 3 cleared the base of part of this cliff, showing an uneven junction of the Pebbly Series with the Chillesford Beds, about 330 yards or so south of the ruined farm. The general evenness of that junction here is noticed above.

At a spot less than 80 yards north of the ruined farm (Easton), and 4 feet down, MR. FRENCH saw, in 1887, a wedge-shaped boulder in the pebbly gravel. In company with MR. A. S. REID he worked this stone out of the cliff, and found that, if square, it would measure 13 × 13 × 19½ inches, a block of most unusual (? unprecedented) size in this formation. MR. REID describes the rock as a micaceous quartzite, and says that the stratification of the gravel was continuous, and not bent round the boulder.

F 2

# APPENDIX 1. WELL-SECTIONS.

FROSTENDEN. New cottage about a quarter of a mile N. of Blomfield Brickyard, or S.W. of the Church. 1879.

From information at the spot.

[Boulder Clay] { Stony clay (mostly)  
Clean clay - } about 56 feet  
Sand - - - - „ 10 „

HENHAM. The Hall.

Sunk and communicated by MR. J. DADE, of Wrentham.

[Boulder] clay - - - - about 26 or 27 feet.  
Gravel and sand, with a little Crag at bottom ? 35 „

To water 61 „

REYDON HALL. 1865.

Information from MR. WILMER.

Soil and sand about 7  
Clay - - „ 3 } 45 feet.  
Crag, very shelly „ 35

The height to which this brings the Crag is more than one would expect : perhaps some part of what is here called Crag may rather belong to the overlying sand or gravel. MR. W. M. CROWFOOT, of Beccles, has a collection of the shells found. (See List, pp. 82, 83.)

SOTTERLY. Brickyard. About 1869.

Communicated by MR. S. V. WOOD, Junr. (from information from workmen in the pit, and from examination of material brought out).

[Glacial Drift] { Red earth, the same as in the pit, with occasional sand galls as big as a small cask. Lower part a little freer from stones 25 feet.  
Yellowish-white sand with small shingle - 4 „  
Chillesford Clay ; with micaceous grains abundant, varies in thickness up to - - - - - 7 „  
Sand, slightly gravelly [Crag] - - - - 4 „

To water 40 „

SOUTHWOLD. Market Place.

Sunk and communicated by MR. J. DADE.

Sand and gravel [Pebbly Series] 45 feet; with about 5 feet of water.

SOUTHWOLD. Waterworks. On the Common. 1886, 1887.

About 40 feet (? more) above Ordnance Datum.

Made and communicated by MESSRS. LEGRAND AND SUTCLIFF. (Notes from an examination of specimens, on the spot, by MR. C. REID) and [Notes by W. W.]

| | THICKNESS. | | DEPTH. | |
|---|---|---|---|---|
| | FT. | IN. | FT. | IN. |
| Ballast [Pebbly Series] - - - | 37 | 0 | 37 | 0 |
| Dark yellow (red) sand - - | 8 | 0 | 45 | 0 |
| Dark yellow, sand (with shells, stained red, *Cardium edule?, Cyprina Islandica, Littorina rudis, Melampus pyramidalis*) - | 33 | 0 | 78 | 0 |
| Dark yellow (red) sand - - | 6 | 0 | 84 | 0 |
| Light-yellow sand with black pebbles (flint and hard veined grit) and shells (*Mya truncata, Tellina obliqua, Littorina littorea*) | 6 | 0 | 90 | 0 |
| Light-grey (silty) sand (full of mica) | 18 | 0 | 108 | 0 |
| Light-greenish blowing sand (the colouring matter seems to be small grains of phosphate, and not glauconite) - - - | 56 | 0 | 164 | 0 |
| Light-greenish loamy sand, with shells (*Pecten opercularis, Natica,* etc.) - - - - | 2 | 0 | 166 | 0 |
| Dark stiff clay (hard, brown) - | 10 | 0 | 176 | 0 |
| Grey loamy sand and shells (sandy silt, with worn shell-fragments. (*Balanus crenatus? Salicornaria crassa,* etc.) - - | 8 | 0 | 184 | 0 |
| Dark clay and stones (soft greenish clay, with harder clay nodules) [specimen light-grey, and light in weight, not like London Clay] - - - - | 1 | 0 | 185 | 0 |
| Dark (brown, hard) clay [a specimen, from the top part?, micaceous, which is not a character of London Clay] - - | 23 | 0 | 208 | 0 |
| Stone [septaria] - - | 1 | 2 | 209 | 2 |
| Dark (brown, hard) clay - - | 6 | 0 | 215 | 2 |
| Stone (septaria) - - | 1 | 0 | 216 | 2 |
| Dark (brown, hard) clay - - | 5 | 0 | 221 | 2 |
| Stone (septaria) - - - | 1 | 4 | 222 | 6 |
| Dark (brown, hard, rather more sandy) clay; in the bottom 10 feet mixed with some very fine glistening sand (a pebble seen, from the bottom, and the foreman said that so few were found that their occurrence was not noted) - - - | 30 | 0 | 252 | 6 |
| Mottled clay [specimen light-grey and red] (Mr. Reid notes black and red) - - - | 10 | 0 | 262 | 6 |
| Dark (greenish) grey loamy sand [specimen, fine, brownish-grey, compact] - - - | 7 | 0 | 269 | 6 |
| Dark clay (hard, mottled dark blue and green, for top 7 feet, rest not seen). [Specimens, dull brown clay, with green specks] - - - | 40 | 0 | 309 | 6 |
| Chocolate-brown clay - - | 5 | 0 | 314 | 6 |
| Greenish sandy clay [specimen dark greenish-grey, at 315] - | 8 | 6 | 323 | 0 |
| Chalk, soft, white, with a few flints - | 256 | 0 | 579 | 0 |

Left-margin bracket labels:

[Crag, 147 feet.]

[London Clay, 68¼ feet].

[Reading Beds, 70½ feet.]

The chalk caved in at this depth; so that no further progress can be made without lining the bore. The water found was small in quantity, and not satisfactory in quality (brackish). The unexpected rise of the Chalk-surface towards Lowestoft, noticed on p. 4, makes infiltration of sea-water a more possible occurrence than would have been thought otherwise; but the saltness of the chalk-water in deep borings near the Essex and Suffolk coast is remarkable.

WRENTHAM. House just N.E. of National School, on the high road, at the edge of the village.

Sunk and communicated by MR. J. DADE.

Sand  -   -   -   - 7 feet.
Brickearth (Chillesford Clay) - 5 „

WRENTHAM? Between cottages, about 1½ miles N.W. of church. Mr. Rockham's. 1880.

Sunk and communicated by MR. J. DADE.

About 60 feet [? Boulder Clay, or chiefly so] to water.

---

The following section, of a well in the southern corner of Suffolk (in Sheet 48 N.E.), came to hand just before this Memoir was sent to press.

FELIXSTOW. Messrs. Bugg and Jolly's second well. 1887.

About 60 feet above the first well, and from 400 to 500 yards from the sea. The first well is described in "The Geology of the Country around Aldborough," etc., p. 56, as "Messrs. Bugg and Colley. At the foot of the cliff between Bent Hill and the Bath Hotel."

Made and communicated by MR. F. BENNETT, of Ipswich.

Shaft 52½ feet, the rest bored, and a tube driven down into the Chalk.

There was some trouble in sinking the brick shaft, owing to the great amount of water met with, beginning at the depth of about 14 feet.

Water stands in the tube 61½ feet below the surface of the ground.

| | | THICKNESS. | | DEPTH. | |
|---|---|---|---|---|---|
| | | FT. | IN. | FT. | IN. |
| Clay [soil, etc.]  -  -  -  - | | 2 | 0 | ¯2 | 0 |
| Sand and Crag [Red Crag]  -  -  - | | 17 | 0 | 19 | 0 |
| [London Clay, about 83½ feet ?] | Blue clay; with rocks [septaria] a foot thick, at 83½ feet, and 7 inches thick, at 89 feet -  - | 82 | 1 | 101 | 1 |
| | Dark loam [basement-bed]  - | 1 | 6 | 102 | 7 |
| | Light [-coloured] stiff clay  - | 6 | 0 | 108 | 7 |
| | Mottled clay  -  -  - | 11 | 0 | 119 | 7 |
| | Very hard rock  -  -  - | 1 | 9 | 121 | 4 |
| [Reading Beds, about 54 feet ?] | Sand loam -  -  -  - | 6 | 0 | 127 | 4 |
| | Mottled clay  -  -  - | 6 | 6 | 133 | 10 |
| | Running sand  -  -  - | 12 | 6 | 146 | 4 |
| | Sand, clay and loam  -  - | 2 | 0 | 148 | 4 |
| | Mottled loam  -  -  - | 3 | 6 | 151 | 10 |
| | Dark brown clay -  -  - | 2 | 6 | 154 | 4 |
| | Mottled clay  -  -  - | 1 | 4 | 155 | 8 |
| | Flint and chalk  -  -  - | 1 | 0 | 156 | 8 |
| Chalk -  -  -  -  -  - | | 243 | 4 | 400 | 0 |

Possibly the London Clay should be carried lower, in which case this section would agree better with the older one.

# APPENDIX 2. LIST OF FOSSILS.

## FROM THE CRAG, FROM THE CHILLESFORD BEDS, AND FROM THE PEBBLY SERIES.

In the column for the Crag the following abbreviations are used :—

B = Bulchamp: Pit near the Union House. This locality is included, though just beyond our district, at the edge of Sheet 50 N.E. (to the west), for the sake of comparison and of getting a more inclusive list. The authority is PROF. PRESTWICH. *Quart. Journ. Geol. Soc.*, vol. xxvii., pp. 344, 483–493.

D = Dunwich cliff (see pp. 52, 53). Authority W. M. CROWFOOT and E. T. DOWSON, *Proc. Norwich Geol. Soc.*, part iii., pp. 81–83. The Mollusca "identified in all doubtful cases by S. V. WOOD."

E = Easton Bavent cliff (see pp. 65, 66). Authority PROF. PRESTWICH, *Quart. Journ. Geol. Soc.*, vol. xxvii., pp. 315, 346, 484–493. Two species added from WOOD, *Ibid.*, vol. xxii., p. 545.

R = Reydon : Well at Hall (see p. 78). On the authority of MR. W. M. CROWFOOT, who tells me that unfortunately "the owner kept only such univalves as he thought at the time were rare."

S = Southwold, cliff N. of town (see p. 61). From a list by S. V. WOOD, JUN. Third Supplement to the Crag Mollusca, pp. 23, 24, *Palæontograph. Soc.*, with some additions on the authority of Mr. W. M. CROWFOOT.

Sw = Southwold Waterworks Well. From specimens got and determined by Mr. C. REID.

Y = Yarn Hill (see p. 15). Authority REV. O. FISHER, *Quart. Journ. Geol. Soc.* vol., xxii., p. 26 ; S. V. WOOD, *Ibid.*, p. 345. (The " Chillesford Beds " here must mean the Crag, as no fossils have been found in the trace of Chillesford Clay at this locality); and PROF. PRESTWICH, *Ibid.*, vol. xxvii., p. 346.

X = Names of some species recorded in the " Catalogue of the Tertiary and Post Tertiary Fossils in the Museum of Practical Geology," pp. 72–74 (1878), as from Southwold. No Crag having been found *at* Southwold until the advent of the Geological Survey, *near* Southwold must be meant, the exact locality being probably Easton Cliff.

---

The list for the Chillesford Beds is derived from one locality, Easton Bavent Cliff. Authority PROF. PRESTWICH, *Quart. Journ., Geol. Soc.*, vol. xxvii., p. 345

---

In the column for the Pebbly Gravel the references are as follows :—

P = Pit on the Lowestoft Road, a little out of Southwold (see p. 29). Species determined by Mr. W. M. CROWFOOT.

St = Southwold Station (see p. 29). Authority S. V. WOOD, Second Supplement to the Crag Mollusca, pp. 52, 53, *Palæontograph Soc.*, with additions by Mr. W. M. CROWFOOT.

---

In all cases the names have been revised by Mr. G. SHARMAN and Mr. E. T. NEWTON.

| | Crag. | Chillesford Beds. | Pebbly Gravel. |
|---|---|---|---|
| **MAMMALS.** | | | |
| Arvicola, teeth - - - | – D. | | |
| Bos, bones - - - | – D. | | |
| Cervus, bone - - - | – D. | | |
| Elephas, bone (and ivory? D.), teeth (E. shore) - | – D. E. | | |
| Equus, tooth - - - | – D. | | |
| Mastodon, teeth - - | – – E. | | |
| Rhinoceros, vertebræ - - | – D. | | |
| Cetacean vertebræ (and rib, D.) - | – D. E. | | |
| **FISH.** | | | |
| Platax Woodwardi, Ag. - - | – – E. | | |
| Raia antiqua, Ag. - - | – – E. | | |
| Ray, spine bone of - - | – | | – St. |
| Fish, fin-bones (D.) and vertebræ - | B. D. E. | | |
| **MOLLUSCA.** | | | |
| *Gasteropoda.* | | | |
| Actæon Noæ, Sby. - - | B. | | |
| „ „ tornatilis, *Linn.* - | B. – E. | | |
| Buccinum Dalei, Sby. - | – – E. – – – – – X. | × | |
| „ undatum, *Linn.* - | B. – E. – – – – Y. | | |
| „ „ var. Grœnlandicum, *Chemn.* | – – E. | | |
| „ „ var. tenerum, Sby. | – – E. | | |
| Bulimus - - - | B. | | |
| Bythinia tentaculata, *Linn.* | B.? | | |
| Calyptræa Chinensis, *Linn.* - | – D. | | |
| Cancellaria viridula, *Fab.* - | – D. | | |
| Cerithium tricinctum, *Brocchi.* - | B. D. – R. S. – Y. | | P. St. |
| Cypræa avellana, Sby. - | B. | | |
| Helix arbustorum, *Linn.* - | – – E. | | |
| „ hispida, *Linn.* - | B. | | |
| „ „ „ var. plebeia, *Drap.* | B. D. | | |
| Hydrobia ulvæ, *Pennant* - | – D. – – S. | | |
| Limnæa limosa, *Linn.* (= L. peregra) | – – E. | | |
| „ palustris, *Müller* - . | B. | | |
| Littorina littorea, *Linn.* - | B. D. E. – S. Sw. Y. – | × | P. St. |
| „ rudis? *Maton* - | – D. – – – Sw. | | – St. |
| Melampus (Conovulus) pyramidalis, Sby. - - | B. D. E. R. S. Sw. | | P. St. |
| Nassa incrassata, *Müller* - | – – – – S. | | |
| „ propinqua, Sby. - | – – E. | | |
| „ reticosa, Sby. - | – – E. | | |
| Natica catena, *Da Costa* - | B. D. E. – – – Y. – | | P.? |
| „ catenoides, *Wood* - | B. – E. – S. – – X. | | |
| „ cirriformis, Sby. - | – – – – – – | × | |
| „ clausa, *Brod.* and Sby. - | – D. – – S. | | |
| „ Guillimini, *Phil.* - | – – – – – Y. | | |
| „ helicoides, *Johnston* - | – D. E. | | |
| „ hemiclausa, Sby. - | B. – – – S.? – – X. | | |
| „ sp. - - | – – – – – Sw. | | – St. |
| Paludina media, *Woodw.* (= P. lenta, *Brander,* and? P.contecta, *Millet*) - | B. D. E. – – – Y. – | | – St. |
| „ parilis, *Wood* - | – – – – – X. | | |
| Planorbis complanatus, *Linn.* - | B. | | |

| | Crag. | Chillesford Beds. | Pebbly Gravel. |
|---|---|---|---|
| Planorbis corneus, *Linn.* - - | B. | | |
| „ spirorbis, *Linn.* - | B. | | |
| Pleurotoma Dowsoni, *Wood* (according to Mr. E. T. Dowson this was recorded by mistake as from Aldeby, by Wood) - | – – R. | | |
| Purpura lapillus, *Linn.* - | B. D. E. - S. – Y. | ⅄ | P. St. |
| „ tetragona, *Sby.* - | – – – – – – X. | | |
| Ringicula buccinea, *Brocchi* - | – – – – – Y. | | |
| „ ventricosa, *Sby.* - | – D. | | |
| Scalaria Grœnlandica, *Chemn.* - | B. - E. – – – - X. | | |
| „ Trevelyana, *Leach* - | B. | | |
| „ sp. - - - | – D. | | |
| Succinea oblonga, *Drap.* - | B. – – – – Y. | | |
| „ putris, *Linn.* | – – – R. | | |
| Trophon antiquus, *Linn.* - | B. D. E. - S. .. Y. | | |
| „ „ var. striatus-contrarius - | – D. | | |
| ? „ gracilis, *Da Costa* | – D. | | |
| Turritella terebra, *Linn* (= T. communis) - | B. D. E. R. S. – – – | × | - St. |
| „ incrassata, *Sby.* - | – – – – S. | | |
| **LAMELLIBRANCHIATA.** | | | |
| Abra alba, *W. Wood* - | -B. | | |
| „ obovalis, *Wood* - | – – - E. | | |
| Artemis lentiformis, *Sby.* - | – – .. – – - - X. | | |
| „ lincta, *Pult.* - | – – E. | | |
| Astarte borealis, *Chemn.* - | – – E. – – Y. | | |
| „ compressa, *Montf.* - | – D. E. - S. | × | |
| „ sulcata, *Da Costa* - | – D. | | |
| „ sp. - - | B. | | |
| Cardita scalaris, *Leathes* - | .. - - | × | |
| „ (derived?) - | – D. | | |
| Cardium edule, *Linn.* - | B. D. E. - S. Sw. Y. | × | P. St. |
| „ Grœnlandicum, *Chemn.* | – D. E?- – – – - | - | - St. |
| Circe minima, *Montf.* - | – - E. | | |
| Corbicula fluminalis, *Müller* | B. D. E. - S. | | |
| Corbula gibba, *Oliv.* - | – – E.? | | |
| „ striata, *Walker* and *Boys* (= C. nucleus) - | B. D. E. - S. – – – | - | - St. |
| „ sp. - | - - - - | × | |
| Cyprina Islandica, *Linn.* - | B. D. E. - S. Sw. Y. - | × | P. St. |
| Donax vittatus, *Da Costa* (= D. anatinus - | B. – – – S. – – – | - | - St. |
| Leda myalis, *Couth.* - | B. - E. – – - Y. X. | × | |
| „ oblongoides, *Wood* - | – D. - - S. | | |
| „ sp. - | – – – – – – | - | - St. |
| Loripes divaricatus, *Linn.* - | – D. | | |
| Lucina borealis, *Linn* | – D. E. - S. – – | × | - St. |
| Mactra arcuata, *Sby.* - | - D. E. | | |
| „ ovalis, *Sby.* - | B. - E. - S. – Y. | × | |
| „ stultorum, *Linn.* - | – D. | | |
| „ subtruncata, *Da Costa* | B. D. E. – – – Y. | × | |
| „ truncata, *Montf.* - | – D. | | |
| Mactra ? sp. - | – – – – – – – | - | - St. |
| Mya arenaria, *Linn.* - | B. D. E. - S. – – – | - | - St. |
| „ truncata, *Linn.* - | B. - E. .. - Sw. | | |
| „ sp. - | – – – – – – | - | P. |
| Mytilus edulis, *Linn.* - | B. D. E. - S. Y. | × | |
| Nucula Cobboldiæ, *Sby.* - | – D. E. | × | |
| „ tenuis, *Montf.* - | – – E. | | |

| | Crag. | Chillesford Beds. | Pebbly Gravel. |
|---|---|---|---|
| ? Panopæa Norvegica, *Spengler* - | B. | | |
| Pecten opercularis, *Linn.* - - | - D. E. - - Sw. | | |
| „ princeps, *Sby.*, var. pseudo-princeps, *Wood* - - | - - E. - - - Y. | | |
| Pholas? - - - - | - - - - S. - - - | - | St. |
| Pinna - - - - - | - - - - - Y. | | |
| Pisidium amnicum, *Müller* - - | B. - E. | | |
| Scrobicularia plana, *Da Costa* (= S. piperata) - - - | B. D. - - S. | | |
| Sphærium corneum, *Linn.* ( = Cyclas corneus) - - - - | B. - E. | | |
| Solen siliqua, *Linn.* - - - | - D. | | |
| Tapes virgineus, *Linn* - - | - D. | | |
| Tellina fabula, *Gronov.* - - | B. - E. | | |
| „ lata, *Gmel.* - - - | B. D. E. - - - Y. - | × | ⎱ P. (one ⎰ St. |
| „ obliqua, *Sby.* - - | B. D. E. - S. Sw.? Y. - | × | ⎰ or other) ⎱ St. |
| „ prætenuis, *Leathes* - - | B. D. E. - S. - Y. - | - | - St. |
| VARIOUS. | | | |
| Balanus crenatus, *Brug.* - - | B. - - - - Sw.? | | |
| Balanus - - - - | - - - - S. | | |
| Crab claw - - - - | B. | | |
| Leaf, impression of - - - | - - - - | - | × |
| Salicornaria crassa,? *Wood.* - - | - - - - Sw. | | |

From our local Crag therefore there are recorded 111 kinds of fossils, or, omitting the two cases in which unnamed species are entered under genera (*Natica* and *Scalaria*) already represented, 109. From the Chillesford Beds there are 19, and from the Pebbly Series 24, or, treating the specifically represented genera (*Natica* and *Mya*) the same as those of the Crag, 22.

It may be some of interest to note the range of the Mollusca through the three geological divisions, that being the only class enough represented for the purpose. This may be best done in a tabular form, as below, in which the figures in brackets represent the numbers purged of mere generic occurrences. The total number of kinds of Mollusca is 102, or, taking out mere generic occurences, 95, though in 3 of these generic occurrence only is noted, without any specific name.

| Crag only. | Chillesford Beds only. | Pebbly Series only. | Crag and Chillesford Beds. | Crag and Pebbly Series. | All three. |
|---|---|---|---|---|---|
| 69 (64) | 3 (2) | 3 (0) | 7 | 12 (10) | 8 |

The following Entomostraca, noted by PROF. T. R. JONES and MR. C. D. SHERBORN as having been found in "Southwold Crag,"[*] probably came from Easton Cliff, no Crag having been found at Southwold except at one small section, which was not seen before the advent of the Geological Survey (see p. 60).

Cythere polyptycha, *Reuss*, new var.　　　Cytheridea elongata *Brady*.
　„　recurata, new sp.　　　　　　„　punctillata *Brady*.
　„　villosa, *Sars*.

# INDEX.

Names prefixed by * are those of places outside the district.

LONDON : Printed by EYRE and SPOTTISWOODE,
Printers to the Queen's most Excellent Majesty.
For Her Majesty's Stationery Office.
[18635.—500.—12/87.]

Clay

*Clay*

SKETCH MAP, SHOWING THE POSITIONS
OF THE SECTIONS
*10 miles to an inch.*

Cowehithe · Line 4

Line 3

Easton Bavent · Southwold

Dunwich // Lines 1 & 2

tony Loam
Boulder (Clay) } GLACIAL
DRIFT.

Sand

and Clay.

PEBBLE SERIES

d with thin
lar
artings } CLASSED WITH
CRAG.

SCALE OF FEET FOR HEIGHTS

80
70
60
50
40
30
20
10
0

SCALE OF FEET FOR DISTANCES

0  50  100  200  300  400  500  600  700  800

ston Brand

INDEX OF COLOURS.

Soil and Recent accumulations along the top of the cliffs.

Glacial Drift, Boulder Clay Sand and Loam

Pebbly Series

Chillesford Beds.

Crag, for the most part decalcified, with doubtful Sand (Dunwich)

Talus along the foot of the cliff.

DANGERFIELD. LITH. 22, BEDFORD ST. COVENT GARDEN.   12 67.152.

Lightning Source UK Ltd.
Milton Keynes UK
UKHW02061524O123
415868UK00007B/883